The Long Goodbye

The Long Goodbye

Carole A. Jones

iUniverse, Inc.
New York Bloomington Shanghai

The Long Goodbye

iUniverse books may be ordered through booksellers or by contacting:

iUniverse
1663 Liberty Drive
Bloomington, IN 47403
www.iuniverse.com
1-800-Authors (1-800-288-4677)

Because of the dynamic nature of the Internet, any Web addresses or links contained in this book may have changed since publication and may no longer be valid.

The views expressed in this work are solely those of the author and do not necessarily reflect the views of the publisher, and the publisher hereby disclaims any responsibility for them.

ISBN: 978-0-595-51388-8 (pbk)
ISBN: 978-0-595-61877-4 (ebk)

Printed in the United States of America

In loving memory
of Tim.

I miss you.

To
Becky, Rachel, and Daniel

I'm proud of you, my warriors.

Contents

Acknowledgements

Chris Horn, I am indebted to you.
Without you, this story would have remained
merely a cathartic personal endeavor
buried in my hard drive.
Thank you for your
encouragement, suggestions, guidance,
prodding, and invaluable editorial expertise.
One of these days we'll actually have to meet in person!

Special thanks to
my mother, Darlene Reints,
my daughter, Becky,
and
Emily King
for your encouragement
and
proofreading skills.
Your willing hearts and keen eyes
were greatly appreciated.

Introduction

o o o o o o o o o o o o o o o o o o o o o o o o o o o o o o o o o o o o o

"Tell it to your children, and let your children tell it to their children, and their children to the next generation."
Joel 1:3

"You'll never guess what happened today."

I could tell by the look on his face that this was going to be good. Interpreting Tim's varied expressions was pretty easy for me, having been an avid student of my husband for more than twenty years. In fact, we often joked that we could read each other's minds.

The expression he wore conveyed the idea that he had received some exciting information that would affect our entire family, and he was very, very pleased to share it with me. His blue eyes were sparkling and he had a "cat that had swallowed the canary" grin on his face. Tim was like every good man in that it gave him great satisfaction to bring happiness to his family.

"I give up," I said as I stepped into his open arms for my afternoon sugar. "What happened?"

"I got a call today from the personnel office at Misawa AFB in Japan. Out of the blue! They want me to come and work for them. It's not a promotion or anything. I'd still be doing the same job. But, I think it would be a better situation for the family. Plus, it's *Japan*, Carole. Just think of it ... another adventure!"

Up to this point in my family's history, life had seemed like a great adventure. We had traveled to exotic places, met interesting people, and even faced natural disasters. We couldn't wait to see what was in store for the next leg of our journey, and Tim would often remark, "We ought to be writing these things down because someday we could write a book." Little did we know that our adventure was about to take a perilous turn that would leave both Tim and I fighting for our lives.

I once read a quote that said there is enough material in every man's life for a novel. Funny, now that I think about it, the author who spoke those words didn't elaborate whether each person's life novel would necessarily be interesting or mind–numbingly boring. At any rate, between the covers of this little tome is my attempt to capture the development of my family's faith, a faith centered on the person of Jesus Christ. I am not an expert or a theologian, but I am a bona fide human being who, like you, is grateful for the good times in life and who struggles to cling to faith during the troubling times.

The writers of the Psalms admonish us to remember and declare the works of the Lord so that future generations will trust and follow Him. I hope that our story exhorts our children, our future grandchildren, and the body of Christ to "hold fast the confession of our hope without wavering …" (Hebrews 10:23) no matter what lies ahead.

This short work is based mostly upon journal entries and a collection of Web mails written during the two years after tragedy struck my family. My prayer for you as you read this book is simply to remember that God is good.

Carole Jones

1

"First Comes Love"

On February 1, 1981, the scales fell from my future husband's eyes, and he noticed me for the very first time. Our first date was in a jacuzzi.

I was lounging in my dorm room at Idaho State University that evening, talking on the phone with my sister, Connie. With Connie living and working a state away in Washington, it wasn't easy keeping up with each other's lives. Every month or so, one of us would call the other to catch up. Inevitably we'd end up discussing the one topic that is foremost in the minds of all young, single women—young, single men.

"So, who are you dating?" she asked.

"Nobody. I'm not dating anyone right now. There is one guy, though, that I would love to get to know better. His name is Tim, and we have a class together. There's just something about him. I don't know how to describe it, but he's different than most of the other guys that I know."

"Did he ask you out on a date yet?" she queried.

"No way. He doesn't even know I'm alive," I said dejectedly. Tim and I had been in class together for at least a month, and he barely noticed me.

At that exact moment, there was a soft knock on my door. "Hang on a second, Connie. Someone's at the door."

Opening the door, I was stunned to see the young man that we'd just been discussing.

"Hi," he said, "I'm Tim Jones. You're Carole, right?"

I managed to nod my head calmly, but internally my emotions and thoughts were out of control. "Oh my gosh! He's standing right here! And he's actually talking to me! Oh, he's so handsome.… what's he doing here? Is he going to ask me out?"

Tim awkwardly apologized, "Hey, I'm really sorry to bother you, but I hurt my hamstring, and I was wondering if you had keys to the training room? I know it's after hours, but I really need to soak my leg in a whirlpool."

1

So, it wasn't exactly a date, but it was close enough for me.

I had been working as a student athletic trainer for the men's athletic program during the school year, and that is where I had first noticed Tim. Late one afternoon I was kneeling on the turf of the indoor stadium taping an ankle when out of the corner of my eye, I observed a very nice pair of masculine, athletic, tanned legs. I glanced up, wondering who belonged to those incredible legs, and found myself looking into the blue eyes of a tall, handsome young runner. He acknowledged my gaze with a smile, said, "Hi," and jogged off.

"Cute," I thought. "Wonder who that was?"

Later on, my boss, Phil, the head athletic trainer, introduced us. I found Tim to be soft spoken and polite, but upon hearing that I thought Tim seemed like a great guy, Phil warned, "Stay away from that one. He's really religious. He's always talking about the Bible."

Come to find out, Tim and I had the same majors and minors, and even though he was an upperclassman and I was a lowly sophomore, we ended up in a class together during the second semester.

The head of our physical education department, Dr. M., led the small class. Doc M. was a great guy and wonderful teacher, but he greatly intimidated me. Because he genuinely enjoyed spirited debates, he often played the devil's advocate during group discussions—and he was notorious for putting students on the spot.

He seemed to enjoy embarrassing me, and I would always crack under the pressure of these debates—my mind would go completely blank, and my cheeks would turn bright red if it was my turn to defend my point of view. Dr. M. would say, "Don't worry, by the time you've finished this class, I'll have taught you not to blush."

Tim became something of a hero to me because no matter what subject came up, he was never embarrassed, never at a loss for words. I remember once that Tim was still espousing his point of view when the class period ended. Dr. M. got up and left the room, and Tim pursued him down the hall, up the stairs, and through the corridors to Doc's office, arguing all the way. This guy definitely had guts and wouldn't back down if he thought he was in the right.

Another time, Dr. M. left town leaving Tim in charge of the class. Tim showed up to teach the class wearing a gray, three-piece suit that made him look very professional and mature. And handsome! I have no idea what he lectured on that day, but he sure looked terrific.

I had a major crush on Tim, so when he asked me to let him into the training room that evening, I had to fight off the urge to yell, "Anything for you!"

Instead I said calmly, "Sure, I'll open up the training room. But could you hang on a second? I'm on the phone with someone."

I gently closed the door, picked up the phone and whispered frantically, "He's here! It's that guy I was just telling you about, Tim Jones—he's standing right outside my door! I've got to go. Call ya later!"

A five-minute walk and a ten-minute whirlpool turned into an hour and a half of sheer bliss. Tim and I really clicked. Conversation flowed so easily that before we knew it, Tim had been in the 110-degree whirlpool for over an hour. He was dripping with sweat, and I finally suggested that he climb out of the tub before he passed out. He walked me back to my dorm, and as we said goodbye, he stood and looked at me as if he'd never seen me before—but now that he noticed, he definitely liked what he saw.

The next evening, Tim strolled down to the cafeteria that connected the men's and women's dormitories. He had a standing policy of never entering the door of the cafeteria if the word "liver" showed up on the menu marquee in any way, shape, or form. The fare of the day for supper? You guessed it. So Tim walked right on past the door and headed for the women's lobby intending to snag a chum before heading off to one of his favorite places to eat—Skipper's Fish and Chips.

I just happened to be sitting in the lobby studying. OK, OK, to be completely honest, I never studied in the lobby. But I decided to conveniently place myself there that evening hoping to run into Tim again. He was one of the resident advisors for the men's dorm, and I knew that he often frequented the RA office, located in our dorm, in the evenings.

Tim came sauntering in with his hands in his pockets heading for the office. When he spotted me, he stopped. He stood thinking for a couple of seconds, then breezed over and asked, "Hey, Carole, have you had dinner yet?"

I said I hadn't. He explained the whole liver predicament and suggested that we both go and get a bite to eat. I thought that was a great idea and floated up to my room to get my jacket while Tim waited for me in the lobby.

Dinner and conversation went on for such a long time at Skipper's that the manager finally had to ask us to leave so he could close up. By this time it was after 10 p.m., so we returned to my dorm where we sat in the lobby talking until 3 a.m.

That became the pattern for the next few weeks. Tim and I would have dinner together, sometimes taking in a movie, and then return to the lobby of my dorm to talk late into the wee hours of the morning.

Phil had been right on about Tim. This guy was extremely passionate about the Bible. Rather than finding that a deterrent, though, I found it quite appealing. I had noticed that there was something different about Tim, and now I knew what it was—a personal relationship with God. On our very first date at Skipper's, Tim had shared openly about the difference Christ had made in His life.

Having been brought up attending a Protestant church, Tim had always assumed that if you believed in God and were a good person that meant you were a Christian. His family faithfully attended church services, and his father, the local pharmacist, had even been an elder at one time.

Although Tim's life looked pretty typical on the surface, in reality there was dissension and strife in their home. Unable to handle the stress, Tim's father* turned to alcohol and drugs. Tim grew up feeling very resentful towards his father and the underlying simmering anger left him with a temper that continually got the better of him. This amazed me because Tim didn't strike me as an angry person at all. In fact, he seemed quite the opposite.

Over the years, Tim's inability to change increasingly frustrated him, and it wasn't until he had gone to college that he discovered a cure. It all began when Tim went to listen to Josh McDowell, a Christian speaker with Campus Crusade for Christ. Josh spoke about the evidence for the resurrection of Christ and Biblical prophecy, all of which captivated Tim's interest. But I think Josh's personal testimony impacted Tim the most.

By this time we had returned to our dorms, so Tim ran upstairs to get his copy of Josh's book, *The Resurrection Factor*. Tim turned to the back of the book and had me read several paragraphs.

"I had a lot of hatred in my life. It wasn't something outwardly manifested, but there was a kind of inward grinding ... The one person I hated more than anyone else in the world was my father. I despised him. To me he was the town alcoholic. If you're from a small town and one of your parents is an alcoholic, you know what I'm talking about. Everybody knew. My friends would come to high school and make jokes about my father ... they didn't think it bothered me. I was laughing on the outside, but let me tell you I was crying on the inside.... After I made that decision for Christ, love from God through Jesus Christ entered my life. It was so strong, I was able to look my father squarely in the eyes and say, 'Dad, I love you.' And I really meant it ..."

—Josh McDowell, *The Resurrection Factor*

Tim said, "Carole, that was me. That was my life until Christ came into it." As Tim began to grow in his relationship with God, he had discovered that only in and through Christ could he find forgiveness for his own shortcomings, and also the ability to forgive his father.

I can remember Tim leaning toward me, gesturing excitedly and talking earnestly about Jesus Christ. Wow! This guy really knew his Bible. I was impressed, although that wasn't Tim's intention. He was completely sincere in his passion for God's Word.

Finally, Tim asked, "So, Carole ... how about you? What's your spiritual background? Have you ever received Christ as your Savior?"

"Um ... I think so ... I mean, I did something like that last year."

I went on to explain that, like him, I had been brought up attending a Protestant church. As I got older, I quit attending church regularly along with the rest of my family. Except for my sister, Connie, who went a little more often than the rest of us, my family only went to church on holidays. I didn't feel like I was missing out on anything, though, as my life had been happy, busy, blessed, and, I thought, fulfilling. Besides, I rarely understood what the reverend was talking about anyway. I believed in God, knew right from wrong, was a patriotic American, and liked apple pie. If that didn't make me a Christian, then what did?

By the time I was sixteen, I began to have a sneaking suspicion that something was missing in my life. I thought it might help if I joined the youth group at church, but the first night I visited there, Barb G., a longtime classmate, informed me that I wasn't a Christian. She was very kind in the way she approached me and was sincerely trying to help, but I became incensed. Who did she think she was? Offended, I left that meeting vowing never to set foot in a church again.

The following year, the week before my high school graduation, an assembly was held to honor the graduating seniors. During the assembly, our guidance counselor quipped, "We ought to name this the Carole Reints Awards Assembly" because I really cleaned up that day. I was the valedictorian, the prom queen, voted the best overall female athlete, and was awarded several scholarships. Pretty heady stuff for a seventeen year old, but as I stood there amongst my family and friends receiving their hugs and congratulations, I remember feeling frightened and empty and lost.

I knew that I was blessed. I knew that I should feel happy. I knew that I should be eagerly anticipating the future, but all I kept thinking was, "What's the point?" The world around me constantly pointed to personal glory and power and popularity as a means of fulfillment. But, if those things left a void, what else was there?

I had tried "church," and that hadn't helped at all, so as I began college at Iowa State University in the fall, I found myself trying even harder to excel. I studied harder, I trained more diligently, and in my perfectionist attempts to become the best possible person that I could be, I began a private battle with anorexia.

To top it off, I was scared. I lived in a huge, rambling old dormitory with a vast labyrinth of hallways, and one day as I was trying to find my way back to my room, I stumbled upon a group of people watching a movie.

The film was captivating and disturbing. It was all about something called Armageddon and the end of the world. The narrator kept quoting the Bible, and while I had never heard any of this before, I figured that if the Bible said it, then it must be true. The end of the world was just around the corner and Jesus Christ was coming back, and even in my ignorance, I knew that I was not ready. I started wondering if Barb G. had been right after all.

A few days later, I was studying alone in my dorm room when someone knocked on my door. Upon opening the door, I found two young ladies who were looking for one of my roommates. Barb, my roomie, happened to be out with her boyfriend, so I offered to take a message. They said they stopped by to talk to her about a Bible study.

At this I exclaimed, "Really? You study the Bible? Would you mind talking to me about it?"

Surprised, they did stay, and that evening I learned about *the God-shaped void that exists in every human heart* that can only be filled by the person of Jesus Christ.

Tim, listening thoughtfully, finally said, "Hey, that's great, Carole. Why don't you come to church with me this Sunday?"

I told him that the last time I went to church my dad had literally picked me up and put me in the car because I had stubbornly refused to go. Church just wasn't for me, but Tim was persistent. After a month of invitations, I finally relented and went.

The first thing that I noticed was that everyone brought their own Bible and that the pastor actually taught from it! It was all so interesting, and the people were fantastic. From that day on, Tim and I studied the Bible together constantly. Tim mentored me, introduced me to all of his friends, and encouraged me to join a ladies' Bible study with a campus ministry.

I think that by the time we had dated two weeks, we both knew that we'd found our soul mate. But even if we'd never become romantically involved, I would have always thanked God for bringing Tim Jones into my life for Tim taught me how to walk with God.

* Years later, Tim's father, Bob Jones, came to live with us on Guam. He gave his heart to Christ—he kneeled down by our couch, asked Christ to come into his life, stood up a brand new creation, and was sober from that moment on. Tim and his dad enjoyed a very close relationship until Bob's death a few years later.

2

"Then Comes Marriage"

Tim proposed in the fall of my senior year, popping the question after dinner at a Chinese restaurant. Two rather large fortune cookies were brought to our table at the end of the meal, and I was surprised to find this message in mine: "Carole, will you marry me? Love, Tim."

I gasped and stammered, "Oh, yes!" to which Tim replied, "Now, look in the other cookie." You guessed it. Tim had made arrangements ahead of time to secretly place my engagement ring in the other tasty morsel. "No big deal," the manager had told him. "We do this all the time!"

Tim had already graduated, and my dad wanted me to finish school, too, before we were married, so we planned our wedding for the following summer.

I think that Tim and I both realized that love and attraction weren't the only makings for a good marriage, so we submitted to pre-marital counseling before we tied the knot. I think the Lord knew, too, what it would take to develop our characters and make our marriage successful. In His wisdom and sovereignty, He banished us to an island 10,000 miles away from all of our family and friends after our wedding.

During one of our final counseling sessions with our friend and pastor, Bill K., we'd begun working through some of our potential problem areas, and Bill had posed the following question: "What are some of the conflicts and troublesome issues that you might face in your marriage?"

Although Tim and I had the same spiritual beliefs, values, and priorities, we were very different in every other way. Tim, always quick witted, answered sarcastically, "How about starvation?"

Tim had been working at a pizza place and selling cutlery on the side, and I was a hotel maid. Although we seemed to have applied everywhere, neither one of us had managed to come up with a teaching position.

Bill said, "Have you ever considered going to Guam?"

We hadn't because, quite honestly, neither of us had even heard of the place before! Bill and his wife, Sue, had lived on Guam when Bill was in the military, and he knew there was always a need for teachers there. So, we applied, got hired over the phone, got married, and nineteen days after our wedding in 1983, we landed on the tropical island of Guam.

I've often joked about how my wonderful hubby took me on the longest honeymoon ever as we spent roughly ten out of the next twelve years in this tropical paradise. It wasn't all kicks and giggles, though, and we would look back on this time as being our formative years in Christ. God changed us and grew us and matured us, and His methodology was not always unabrasive or painless.

Much like a lapidary grinding off the jagged, irregular edges of a gem in the rough, God used our marriage relationship and our jobs to define, shape, and hew us into the desired form. The basic shape fleshed out, and He then began using our circumstances, and eventually even our children, in a sanding and finishing process that continues through today. He perfected and polished persistently, relentless in an effort to achieve His ultimate objective—that being a mirror-like finish that allows Him to see His own reflection in our lives.

We nearly drove each other crazy the first few months we were married. I was a "cleany," Tim was a "messy." I was an early riser, Tim a night owl. I stomped around our little apartment slamming shut drawers and cupboards that Tim hadn't bothered to close, while he simmered in the bathroom trying to get toothpaste out of a tube that I had squeezed in the middle—again.

Minor irritations often escalated into major arguments, and it was a good thing that we had decided in premarital counseling never, ever to use the "D" word in our marriage, or one of us might have threatened to leave early on. Guam was a tiny island, so we couldn't avoid each other, and our families were too far away to run home to mommy. At three dollars a minute, even long distant phone calls to mom were out, so that forced the three of us—God, Tim, and me—to work things out.

Another thing we had decided in counseling was to live within our means and to stay out of debt. The entire first year we were married, we rode his and her mopeds while we saved up to buy a car. Nothing took the wind out of our sails faster than one of us stomping out the door in a huff after an argument to hop on our "hog" and tear off down the road at a blistering 30 mph. We looked ridiculous, and we knew it.

Realizing we were stuck with each other, we eventually talked through all of these issues. We finally concluded that even with all of our differences, God knew what He was doing when He brought us together. Being opposites in so many ways made us the perfect complement for each other's strengths and weaknesses. Where I was overly reactive and emotional, Tim was more stable and unemotional. I was organized and meticulous to the point of being compulsive and controlling, and Tim was more of a laid-back procrastinator. We were able to learn from and rub off on each other. Over time, we were pulled from our extremes until our personalities and characters were more central and balanced. Sometimes I think that's part of what the Bible means about becoming one. Together, Tim and me made one pretty special person.

Tim and I both taught at the same high school our first few years on Guam. This was in the days before spirituality became so politically incorrect. We were open about our faith and even led a Bible study during our lunch hour. Kids and educators alike knew where we were coming from, and I wish I could say we were beloved for it. Most of our peers and students did love us, and we've kept in touch with several of them to this day, but others despised us, and their antipathy would eventually come back to haunt us.

For example, Tim was hired a few years later as the school's part-time athletic director. Part of his job was to keep abreast of the academic progress of his athletes. One afternoon after doing grade checks, he became aware that one of his student aides, the best female athlete in the school, had become ineligible to play sports due to a low grade point average. The coach of the tennis team was in a class at the local college at the moment, and Tim was unable to contact her (if only cell phones had been invented), so he went to the athlete as she was leaving for her tennis match and explained the situation. She was really disappointed but promised not to play. However, she got caught up in the heat of the competition at the match and ended up playing and leading her team to victory.

As soon as Tim realized what had happened, he called the island sports commission and forfeited the game. The commission, led by several of the educators who didn't particularly like us, decided to fire Tim from his job, stating that he knowingly allowed an ineligible athlete to play and then tried to cover it up. We also found out, too, that the folks responsible for firing Tim had been looking for an opportunity to get rid of him for years.

This shocking turn of events devastated me, but Tim merely took it in stride. He said, "Carole, first of all, look at what is going on in our lives right now." Tim had just been nominated for a leadership position at our church, and he felt that his dismissal at work was a meager attempt by the enemy to ruin his reputation.

"Secondly, look at how God has used this situation!" As a result of the controversy, all the local newspapers interviewed Tim, and he used the opportunities to testify about his faith in God. He'd even been part of a panel discussion on a TV show, and we were later told that nine out of ten callers said they believed Tim was innocent and had been unjustly treated.

There were good days and bad days in our chosen profession. Bad days would include conflicts and run-ins with fellow educators, parents, and students over anything from the color of our skin to spiritual issues. We'd never been a minority before, and often the young, male Chamorro students in our charge resented us telling them what to do. We were threatened more than once, and often not idly. I remember standing on the soccer field alone after class one day cautioning one young man about his disruptive behavior, when he leaned in very close and quietly sneered, "You better watch yourself, lady. You better watch your house, your car, and your family."

Slightly scared, I went looking for Tim who basically offered to remove the lad's head from his shoulders if he ever thought about following through on his threat. The kid left me alone, but the following year we read in the paper that this same young man had robbed and murdered a sailor outside a bar and had been sentenced to life in prison.

Tim and I were strict and had expectations for our students that were not unreasonable. We taught health and physical education, not rocket science, and the only way that a student could fail our class was to sleep through every period or not show up at all. Several students did fail, and more than once Tim and I were pressured by the administration or some parent to pass a student who hadn't made any effort whatsoever.

We both chafed and complained about these unjust situations and fumed at the irritating people that we encountered on a daily basis, but eventually, God's word got through to us.

Once I was sitting in a Bible study when another lady pointed out that from the moment of birth, most people are on a slow and steady march to hell. She said people were deceived and blind and lost and didn't know any better—no wonder they acted the way that they did. Like the Ninevites of the Old Testament who were only days away from God's wrath and punishment, few human beings knew their right hands from their left. Her words really penetrated my heart, and I asked God to begin helping me to see people the way that He saw them.

"Do not allow yourself to be troubled and perplexed when you see people being unreasonable and unjust. Rest in peace in the bosom of God. He sees it all the more clearly than you do, and yet He permits it. Those who injure us are to be loved and welcomed as the hand of God ... Let them do as they will. Just be sure that you see

only God in them. They could do nothing to you without His permission. So, in the end, it is He who tests or blesses us, using them as we have need."
—Fenelon, 17th-century Archbishop to Louis XIV, "Let Go"

I wish I could say that we loved teaching, but it was a hard road. Tim tried more than once to join the military to escape from teaching, but time and time again, he would be minutes away from swearing in and the whole thing would fall through. It was obvious that God wanted us right where we were for the moment, and eventually we decided that, pleasant or unpleasant, our temporal affairs were to be treated merely as fodder for God's obedience program.

Still, there were some highlights from those years. Lighter moments included arming our health education students with facts and information to use as ammunition in refuting the theory of evolution being taught in their biology class. The kids would return to class the next day, excited about the lively debates that had ensued, and more than once, Pat P., a good friend who taught biology, would find Tim and me in the hallway and laughingly say, "Hey, cut it out you guys!"

Tim enjoyed success coaching the school's track and cross-country teams. He really had a way with his runners. They loved him because he knew how to bring out the best in them, and they loved me for the brownies I would bake for them after their long runs on Saturday morning.

The absolute best part about teaching, though, was Carole H., Jenny, Dan, Genevieve, Cynthia, Denise, Pat, Clarence, Henry, and several others whose names now escape my memory. These were some of the students that we had the opportunity to lead to Christ.

3

"Then Comes Carole With a Baby Carriage"

After three years on Guam, we were ready to go home. Tim and I applied to grad school, and the day we found out we were accepted and hired as grad assistants was the same day that we found out that we were expecting a baby. April 15, 1986—a real red-letter day all the way around. It was also Tim's birthday, and the day that the United States bombed Libya.

We returned to Idaho, and while Tim went to school, I stayed home and started punching out little Joneses like movie tickets. Rebecca came along in December 1986, followed quickly by Rachel in June 1988. Having children was the best thing for our walks with God. Our girls softened our hearts and rough edges even further and made us more real than ever before. You can fool some of the people some of the time, but you can't fool your child. They watch every area of your life meticulously, and if your not walking what your talking, they'll spot the hypocrisy a mile off.

We both felt that the children were a gift from God. They were really His children on loan to us for a brief lifetime, and we needed to eventually return them to Him and render an accounting. We tried to make Deuteronomy 6: 5–9 our way of life:

"You shall love the Lord you God with all your heart and with all your soul and with all your might. These words, which I am commanding you today, shall be on your heart. You shall teach them diligently to your sons and shall talk of them when you sit in your house and when you walk by the way and when you lie down and when you rise up. You shall bind them as a sign on your hand and they shall be as frontals on your forehead. You shall write them on the doorposts of your house and on your gates."

We saturated ourselves and our kids in God's word, reading, singing, studying, and praying together over the years. Becky and Rachel, and, eventually, Daniel, who was born in 1992, really didn't know any other way of living.

I was blessed to be a stay at home mom, but getting by financially wasn't easy.

At one time, Tim and I began doing a Larry Burkett Bible study on finances. We tried to set up our budget according to the formula that was suggested, but our income and fixed expenses didn't compute. As a teacher, Tim received two paychecks per month—one entire paycheck plus half of the other went towards paying our rent and utilities. The rest of his check barely covered groceries and basic necessities, and then the money was all gone.

There were some anxious moments, but our circumstances didn't depress us. Actually, they had the opposite effect. We realized that we shouldn't be making it on our meager income, and yet year after year went by with every bill paid. More than once, the end of the year came and we scratched our heads in amazement as we did our taxes. We had a roof over our head, food on the table, clothes on our back, and if not our wants, at least every real needed provided. How come we weren't in debt up to our ears? Our lives were simply a demonstration of God's amazing grace. He provided for us on a daily basis and our children learned firsthand that there was a God who really cared for them and was attentive to their prayers. Even in little things, He was gracious.

I could tell you story after story about how God provided for my family. There was the time I specifically asked God, and only God, for pretty dresses for our girls, only to be given ten the very next day. Or there was the time that our family prayed for a replacement for our worn out van and was given a car. Not just any car either, but a Lincoln Towne car!

There's another story about a Christmas tree that our family still talks about today. We were eating dinner one evening a few weeks before Christmas. Becky was four and Rachel was three. It was the first year that both girls were old enough to comprehend and get wrapped up in all the excitement of the season. Becky wanted to know if we were going to decorate a tree. Unfortunately, even a tiny Charlie Brown type Christmas tree cost around fifty dollars, and things were so tight at the moment we couldn't afford both a tree and presents for the girls.

Disappointed, the girls understood the situation. Still, Becky, who was used to praying for everything, insisted that we stop immediately and ask God to provide a Christmas tree. Tim tried to gently tell her that Christmas trees probably weren't a priority for the Lord at the moment, but we bowed our heads anyway as little Becky prayed something like, "Jesus, could we please have a Christmas tree this year?"

Now, this is the honest truth ... we opened our eyes, and as we started to eat our meal, there was a knock on the apartment door. Tim answered it and there stood one of the other elders from our church, Ed P.

Ed said, "Every year I buy a Christmas tree for the pastor. Well, the pastor is new this year and didn't know that I was going to buy one for him, so he already had a tree when I showed up. Anyway, I've got this tree downstairs in my truck. Do you want it?"

Our mouths fell open in amazement, but Becky merely said, "See?" It seemed that stuff like this was always happening to us.

I don't want to make it sound like every prayer we prayed was answered with a resounding "Yes!" We got used to dealing with disappointments, too. After grad school, for example, Tim didn't get a teaching position, so we ended up living in Michigan with his mom for nearly a year. Tim searched and searched for a job to no avail. That was probably the most depressing period of his life. We finally moved back to Guam again—the only place it seemed Tim could get a full-time job in teaching. We often wondered if there had been something the Lord intended for us to learn the first time around that had we missed! We struggled along financially, and I know Tim wished for a better life for his family.

Living within our means meant sacrificing, so our family lived in a tiny, run-down, one-bedroom apartment for several years. It was so small that we often joked to people that if they had more than three people in their family we could never have them over for dinner because they wouldn't fit in our apartment! We drove junky cars, clipped coupons, shopped sales, and lived very basically and simply—and very happily, I might add. Contentment is a learned behavior, and God gave us plenty of practice in that area.

The island of Guam was gorgeous. Spectacular sunny beaches ran alongside tepid bluish-green bays. Lush green jungles lined the roads, their contents so aromatic that we often drove around with our windows down just to smell their sweet fragrance.

There were drawbacks to living in paradise, however—typhoons and earthquakes.

Guam usually experienced several earthquakes a day, but most were so slight that you never even noticed them. Occasionally, one would be strong enough to detect, and even though they lasted only moments, I thought that earthquakes were scarier than typhoons. It was so unsettling to be hit without warning by something of such great force. Typhoons were powerful and scary, too, but at least you knew days in advance that one was coming.

One Sunday evening, we were sitting in the church sanctuary watching a Billy Graham movie. Suddenly, there was a low rumbling sound. It sounded as if a train was approaching, but we knew that this couldn't be as there was no railway on the island. Pretty soon, the pews began to tremble, and we realized all at once that an earthquake had started.

Most earthquakes on Guam were over almost before you knew what was happening, so no one was unduly alarmed as the building jittered and quivered. After about 30 seconds, though, we realized that this quake wasn't about to stop. Things went abruptly from bad to worse. The church was plunged into total darkness and the enormous steel building perched on top of a cliff overlooking the ocean began lurching violently. People began diving for cover, afraid that the roof and walls would collapse on top of them at any moment.

Becky was sitting with us, but Daniel was across the parking lot in the nursery, and Rachel was downstairs in another building. Tim and I never spoke a word, but we each instinctively got up and started heading for a different child.

I remember thinking that we had to get to the kids. I truthfully thought that we were all going to die, and I wanted to make sure that we all went to heaven together. I tripped and stumbled my way across the parking lot, the ground literally rolling like the waves of an ocean. Carrying Rebecca, I often had to pause to regain my balance. As I did, I looked around incredulous to see the cars in the parking lot bouncing two feet off the ground. Huge palm trees and concrete power poles nearly three feet in diameter were scattered around the church grounds swaying dangerously as if they were the pendulums of a clock. It was the longest two minutes of our lives.

Miraculously, no one was killed during the earthquake, which measured 8.2 on the Richter scale. Absolutely amazing—and I later read an article that said the Japanese spent the next year trying to figure out how we came through unscathed.

The Japanese weren't the only ones learning lessons. Every life experience on Guam, and then later in Arizona, that we went through forged in us a real and deepening faith in God.

Why tell you all this? After all, this book isn't meant to be a biography. We're certainly not famous celebrities giving you a behind the scenes look at our private lives. We're just your average American Christian family with the same hopes, dreams, cares, and needs as the rest of humanity. Who cares about us anyway?

Simply put, God does, and in His sovereignty the years spent in college or grad school in Idaho, and then teaching on the island of Guam, were specific preparation for what was to come. Hindsight is 20/20 and I can easily look back at each change of location, each new acquaintance made, and even Tim's eventual change of career where he began working for the military in Guam and Arizona, as a part of God's intricate plan and necessary work for our lives that would eventually carry us through the deep waters that were still to come. Isn't it incredible to know that our lives are not insignificant or happenstance?

In every trial and tribulation, we learned to see not coincidences or random happenings, but the powerful and protective hand of a sovereign God who ruled over our lives. In every need, we saw not what we lacked, but the faithful provision from the hand of a loving Father.

We came to realize that pressure was good as long as it pressed us closer to the Lord's heart. Tim's constant prayer became, "Lord, help us to know You and to know Your word. Not that we would become smart, but that we would be changed into the likeness of Jesus Christ. Stretch us continually, Lord, that we might not grow complacent and lazy in our relationship with You. Mold us, mature us, and fit us for heaven."

God's word says if we ask anything according to His will, we will receive that which we have requested. That's why we don't blame God for what eventually occurred in our lives in the years to come. After all, we sort of asked for it!

4

"Bracing for Colder Winds"

"The results from your biopsy came in today," Dr. Shackleford said over the phone, "and it is breast cancer."

She tried to sound positive as she explained the specifics: invasive mammary carcinoma … smallish tumor … not highly aggressive … appeared the tumor had been removed … more surgery needed … lymph nodes needed to be checked … margins appeared clear.

"All good signs," she said calmly, and I tried to believe her. But, honestly, when she said, "You have cancer," I felt that I had really heard, "You're going to die."

I tried not to fall apart, but I was trembling as I got off the phone.

Strange, but somehow I had known to expect bad news. It had taken two weeks for the results of my biopsy to return to Japan and during that time I had surfed the Internet daily looking up information on the disease with a growing sense of foreboding.

Turning around, I came face to face with the anxious eyes of our oldest daughter, Becky, who had caught the tail end of my conversation.

"Mom, what's the matter? What'd the doctor say?"

I pulled her into my arms, hoping that my warm, familiar embrace would somehow ease the pain of what I had to say.

"I have …" I said falteringly, "I have … cancer."

Cancer. Not a difficult word to pronounce and one which I had spoken easily many times before. Saying it for the first time in reference to myself had taken a

Herculean effort, though, and made this surreal situation seem less dreamlike. Becky's face wasn't visible, but I could feel her small frame quivering, could hear the stifled sobs. Where were my tears, I wondered?

◆   ◆   ◆

Ordinarily when a woman discovers a lump in her breast, she is naturally apprehensive. But in January of 2000 when I discovered a small, hard mass in my right breast, I was not overly concerned. Since my early twenties, I had been plagued with pebbly, often painful, little lumps in both of my breasts—called fibrocystic syndrome—which had culminated in two biopsies. Both times the outcome was normal, although after the last biopsy my surgeon had said something to the effect that, "he hadn't seen the last of me." Ominous words.

Finding a lump was not a new thing and I knew what to do—make my doctor aware of the situation at my next appointment and watch for any changes. Later that spring, I did make my doctor aware of the mass. Unfortunately, he could not feel what I was feeling. He commented, "Just keep an eye on it," which I did. Almost imperceptibly it grew so that by the following spring, the doctor finally noticed it. Following an ultrasound, which just happened to show a cyst in the same area where I felt a lump, I was sent to a new surgeon.

One of my former surgeons, the one who had had premonitions about me, had since moved his practice. I had been such a difficult case that I often wondered if I was the reason he left town. Surgeons were now using a new, less invasive technique to perform most breast biopsies. The outpatient procedure was really quite novel and ideally took only 30 minutes. For some reason, though, this painless, brief procedure usually ended up turning into a painful and frustrating three-hour ordeal for the doctor and me. I was not exactly sure why I was such a problem, but once overheard the doctor muttering something like, "It's like trying to do a biopsy on a brick."

During the last biopsy two and a half years ago, the radiologist tried to explain some of the difficulty to me. She said, "Honey, trying to read your mammogram is like trying to read something through a brick wall on a pitch black night with no moon and no stars. Problem areas on mammograms show up as white spots—your mammograms are like vanilla ice cream! Everything is white. We can't see a thing."

The radiologist at my very first biopsy was an impatient man. He took one look at my mammogram, and with a frustrated shake of his head said abruptly, "If you were my wife, I'd tell you to have double prophylactic mastectomies right away." I laughed incredulously, "You're not serious, are you? I mean, come on—you don't just start lopping off body parts because you're afraid that you're going to get cancer."

He said, "I'm very serious. You're a walking nightmare. Your tissue is so dense that you could have a cancer somewhere in there and we might never, ever find it." Looking back, he was prophetic.

Subsequently, one can only imagine my glee in hearing this new surgeon pronounce me free to go this time. Everything was fine and there was no need to subject me to a difficult biopsy. My most recent mammogram had been "normal" for me and since there was a cyst in the area, the surgeon decided that was the problem. I promised him that I would continue to get my yearly mammogram (due in July) and went merrily on my way.

But, life had gotten busy. Tim had begun working for the military while we still lived on Guam, and we'd eventually been transferred to Luke AFB in Phoenix when our base on Guam closed in 1995. Just recently Tim had accepted a position as the base Fitness Program Manager for Misawa AFB. We relocated to Japan that summer of 2001, and in all the bustle of moving, I forgot to get my next mammogram. Months passed and the "cyst" in my breast became more and more prominent. The surgeon had said it might get larger, but Tim was becoming concerned and often asked me to see a doctor again. Finally, he pulled rank and said jokingly, "Listen, if you don't go to a doctor pretty soon I'm going to start quoting scriptures about submission. Didn't our marriage vows say something about promising to love and *obey* me? Honey, please make an appointment."

Laughingly, I replied, "Yes, master," and obeyed.

Several weeks later, I watched the smile vanish from my new doctor's face as he examined the lump. "I wouldn't feel right letting you leave here without setting up an appointment with a surgeon. Just to be on the safe side," he said.

We scheduled the appointment, and meanwhile I got another mammogram. The radiologist said, "You will most definitely need to see a surgeon." He went even further and said, "And, you'll definitely need a biopsy." I had just turned 40, just had my gall bladder removed, was feeling really, really tired, and now I was being sent to a surgeon for another biopsy. I wasn't afraid, but I was beginning to wonder if, maybe, my warranty had expired?

The first time we met with the surgeon she attempted a fine needle aspiration of the cyst hoping that that would eliminate the problem. After several attempts, she finally paused and with a quizzical look on her face said, "Hmm, no fluid. It's a solid mass. We need to biopsy this."

I sat there stunned as her words sunk in and a feeling of dread slowly crept over me. The mass was not a cyst? What in the world had I been walking around with for over two years? Something was terribly wrong. At that moment I think I knew that I had cancer.

I had had the exact same feeling years ago right before my older sister, Connie, was diagnosed with cancer. My family was residing on Guam at the time and had no idea that 32-year-old Connie had found a lump in her neck which turned out to be cancerous. Not only that, but the cancer had already metastasized throughout her lymph system. Her doctors called her an aberration—Connie had not one single risk factor or even a symptom. Even worse, they could not find the origin of her cancer. She was young, athletic, vibrant, and healthy—and dying of an unknown cancer. Sadly, we lost her 16 months later.

I believe that the apprehension that I began to feel at that moment was the Holy Spirit trying to prepare me to hear the words, "You have cancer." Still, the news impacted me like a physical blow and left our family reeling for days. Tim immediately fired off an e-mail to everyone that we knew and asked for prayer support. Hundreds of people began to entreat the Lord on our behalf and within a few days, we began to feel the effects of that intercession. We calmed down and quit crying as a supernatural peace and strength began to permeate our lives.

Tim was convinced that this physical crisis was actually a spiritual attack. God's word indicates in several places that physical illness is sometimes brought about due to the actions of Satan (as in the case of Job) or his minions. Luke 13:11–16 makes mention of a woman *"who for eighteen years had had a sickness caused by a spirit … "*

I do not know whether or not that was the case with me, but I did not pace around the house asking the Lord, "Why me?" I had already answered that question in my heart with, "Why NOT me?"

Early on in my relationship with God, I probably would have hurled the big "why" question at the Lord because I had been under the impression that once I had eternal life, everything would be rosy. After all, that's what the tracts say, right? *"God loves you and has a wonderful plan for your life."* (Oh goody, I can hardly wait!) So, when life started to dish out disappointment after disappointment, I said to myself, "Did I miss the fine print somewhere? What's going on?" My thinking, I found out, was not scriptural.

The lives of Job, Joseph, and the numerous believers mentioned in Hebrews Chapter 11 were just a few examples in the Bible that testified to the difficulties Christians faced in their lifetimes.

"In this you greatly rejoice, even though now for a little while, if

necessary, you have been distressed by various trials." 1 Peter 1:6.

"Consider it all joy, my brethren, when you encounter various trials, knowing that the testing of your faith produces endurance." James 1:2

Just a smattering of the verses in the Bible that alluded to the trials that the early Christians had faced and foreshadowed what future saints could expect. Christ's very words before He went to the cross were, *"These things I have spoken to you, so that in Me you may have peace. In the world you will have tribulation, but take courage, I have overcome the world." John 16:33*

We've been warned!

"It is not part of the Christian hope to look for a life in which a man is saved from all trouble and distress; the Christian hope is that a man in Christ can endure any kind of trouble and distress, and remain erect all through them, and come out to glory on the other side."
—William Barclay

We have all heard someone say, "I've got some good news for you, and some bad news." The bad news for God's children is that not only are we not home, but we are presently living in a war zone. God expects us to occupy hostile enemy territory until He comes for us. In the meantime, things are bound to get tough and it shouldn't surprise us to see casualties of war.

But, the good news is that we are never abandoned. God promises to be with us in every hard situation.

"For He Himself has said, "I will never desert you, Nor will I ever forsake you," so that we confidently say the Lord is my helper, I will not be afraid. What will man do to me?" Hebrews 13:5–6

We are also promised that whatever befalls us will ultimately result in our good.

"And we know that God causes all things to work together for good to those who love God, to those who are called according to His purpose." Romans 8:28

Our lives, including any suffering that we endure, have a purpose and fit into a divine plan.

I had come to the conclusion, after reading books such as *Foxe's Book of Martyrs* that during times of severe testing, God's children were given a special portion of His grace, power, strength and peace. How else can one explain the calm demeanor that saint after saint had displayed throughout history while meeting their demise in some of the most horrific ways known to mankind? Believers, one after another, praising God as they were consumed by flames, or just as bad, by wild animals. Frail human beings subjected to ingeniously cruel methods of torture and termination boldly preaching the gospel until their lips were silenced forever.

"Lord," I often wondered, "What would it be like to face an extreme test of faith like that? Would my faith stand firm?" Keeping all this in mind helped me not to feel picked on. Instead, I felt picked out!

Meanwhile, decisions needed to be made. I would need additional surgery, and then depending on the outcome, possibly further treatment. Misawa AFB did not have the resources to treat cancer, and it became apparent that we would need to return to the states.

So many questions remained. How extensive was the cancer? Where should we seek treatment? Should we relocate permanently or temporarily? I was over-whelmed by it all, but, fortunately, Tim was not. He felt that we should return to Phoenix.

Hopefully, the only treatment I would require would be a little more surgery, but if not, Tim could exercise his return rights to his former job at Luke AFB and our family would move back to Arizona. We had only lived in Misawa for a year, and most of our friendships were fairly new. Still, we were inundated with sup-port and love. We marveled at how our crisis had given these blossoming rela-tionships a violent shove into intimacy.

The kids were left in Japan for the time being in the very loving, capable hands of our friends, Robb and Merry D. Joel, Melody, and Bethany, their kids, were already fast friends with our children. Our former church family in Phoenix was poised and standing by to help Tim and me when we arrived in the states.

On August 29, after arriving in Phoenix, I recorded this entry in my journal: *"We are in AMAZING spirits. Obviously this isn't coming from inside of us—just another manifestation of God's grace. Right now we are at Steve and Tami's (pastor and wife)—what a great brother and sister. They have graciously opened their home and hearts to us. A family from church has lent us one of their cars. What a blessing. Many others have encouraged us. Lord, thank you for the body of Christ. I am grateful that in Your wisdom You created such a thing and placed me in it. Here I am, such a tiny part, and yet when wounded, the entire body becomes provoked, rushing in to help, heal, comfort and protect.*

Tim and I have come to a decision. I am going to have bilateral mastectomies; I don't want to have to go through this ever again. Thank you, Lord, for my wonderful husband's support, strength, and unconditional love.

Tim is my hero. He said again today that the only thing that mattered to him was that I was around for the next 40 years—not my physical appearance. I know he means it. I pray that you will lead us to the right surgeon, that the cancer has not metastasized, and that I'll be healed and home soon."

5

"Battle Plan"

We began meeting with surgeons over the next couple of days. One of the surgeons we met, Dr. Z., had performed my very first biopsy years ago. Strictly a breast surgeon, he was well known throughout the valley for his skill. We vaguely remembered liking the guy, and after meeting with him again, we realized why. Dr. Z is a wonderful, compassionate human being with a great bedside manner.

After presenting my case we were ushered into one of the exam rooms where we waited for more than a half hour. Tim was on the verge of becoming annoyed when suddenly the doctor returned, apologizing profusely, "Sorry about the delay, but I had two other patients scheduled that I needed to see quickly. I don't have any other appointments for the rest of the afternoon, so now we can take all the time that we need. I can concentrate on you, and no one will disturb us."

Then, he spent the next two hours talking with us. We were impressed and soon realized that we were not the only ones to hold him in high regard. During the course of my treatment, whether I was getting lab work done, having X-rays taken, or checking into a hospital, everywhere I went I heard the same thing. "Dr. Z. is your doctor? Oh, he's a wonderful person. He's so nice!"

Inevitably, too, if a woman had made the comment, she would add, "And he's so handsome."

We heard this statement so many times during my treatment that to this day, my family refers to this genial man as "Dr. Z. He's So Nice" as if that were his entire name.

Although the primary concern for everyone was my health and eliminating the cancer, it was also important that I end up with a decent cosmetic result. The doctor finally said, "I don't think you'll be happy with the results of a lumpectomy. If you were a larger woman, a lumpectomy might not be very noticeable, but as it is …"

25

This was his very diplomatic way of saying that not enough of my 102 pounds had made it into my bra. I told him that I'd already decided against a lumpectomy anyway.

"I've been reading and I suspect that I'm genetically predisposed to get cancer," I said. "I mean, really, how often do two perfectly healthy sisters with zero risk factors develop cancer unless it has something to do with their genes? If that's the case, then I am much more likely to get cancer in the other breast as well."

"Considering the difficulty in finding the cancer the first time around, I'd just as soon eliminate the problem before it becomes a problem. I'd like you to do bilateral mastectomies. My surgeon in Misawa thought that my 'pre-emptive strike theory' was way too drastic—what do you think?"

"No, I don't think it is drastic. You're young and you have a lot of years left to live, so your objective should be to get the risk of recurrence as close to zero as possible," he said.

The decision was made. I have had the privilege of meeting many breast cancer survivors during the past two years, and I've been amazed at how each woman has selected a course of treatment that was just as unique as the woman receiving it. I was grateful to be living in an era where so many options were available.

After meeting with Dr. M., the plastic surgeon, I was even more grateful. He showed Tim and me photos of some of his clients who had received the same reconstructive surgery that I would be having.

"They're so beautiful. Every single woman looks better than she did before!" I said in amazement. "You must feel wonderful about what you do, making something beautiful come out of something tragic."

Dr. M. was a very kind professional who had a businesslike manner, but I saw his demeanor soften dramatically as he smiled and replied, "It is so gratifying. I love what I do."

A date for surgery was set. September 12—almost two weeks away! Just enough time to get really homesick and really nervous. Tim and I tried unsuccessfully to act like we were on vacation. We took in a movie or two and went out to dinner, but neither one of us felt very festive with our little black cloud of uncertainty following us everywhere we went. The biggest question would remain unanswered until a few days post-surgery. Had the cancer spread?

Tim, full of optimism from the start, believed without a doubt that I was going to be just fine and refused to discuss any other opinions. So, I didn't share with him that I had a feeling that the cancer had spread into my lymph nodes. True, the cancer was slow growing and not highly aggressive, but I'd had an invasive cancerous tumor in my breast for over two years. It seemed highly unlikely to me that it hadn't reached the nodes.

The hardest part of the whole experience thus far was being apart from the children. We held off bringing Becky, Rae, and Daniel over from Japan, planning to wait until we had learned the outcome of the surgery. Robb and Merry D. and Bobbi and Dennis C. and their families were actively ministering to our kids, keeping their spirits up, but with each phone call, there was increasing evidence that a meltdown had begun to occur.

I called one evening expecting to hear about Daniel's daily shenanigans with his accomplice, Bethany, but instead of his usual animated chattering, I got a prolonged silence. "Dan, are you still there?" More silence. "How are you, pal?" Finally, a sound. Stifled sniffles. My little boy, tired of being brave, confessed mournfully, "Mommy, I really, really miss you and Daddy. When are we coming to the states?" It was time to send for them.

Before we could make the arrangements, though, Dennis called to inform us that he'd found a screaming deal on plane tickets.

"The tickets are booked and paid for, and a plan has been formed," he said. "It's a done deal. The kids will arrive in Phoenix on the 18th." Evidently, God had put a burden on the hearts of several of our friends in Japan—they had all pitched in and bought plane tickets for our kids! Our hearts were so blessed by this generous demonstration of love, and we, once again, saw our amazing, able God provide for a need that we had not even expressed out loud.

September 11, 2002

"Though He slay me, yet I will hope in Him." Job 13:15

What we have come for, what we have been waiting for has finally arrived. Tomorrow is the surgery. I pray for courage. I know that I don't have it in me to be fearless, but I trust God to supply what I lack from His inexhaustible resources. I don't like pain and the unknown makes me fearful, so I will try to focus on what I do know: God is good and He loves me. He not only lives in the present, but in the future, too. My future. He loves me—proved that beyond a shadow of a doubt on the cross over 2000 years ago, and He has demonstrated it every day of my life since I received Christ as my Savior. There is no limit to His power, His wisdom, His mercy, His kindness. His loving kindness reaches higher than the heavens. He promises to be with me and to give me His peace, "not as the world gives … Do not let your heart be troubled, nor let it be fearful." John 14:27

6

"In the Trenches"

The day of surgery was uneventful. I don't remember much after my visit with the anesthesiologist, a.k.a., The Sandman. Neither Tim or I were the least bit fearful or anxious. Beaming, my team of doctors boasted that the surgery couldn't have gone better. Dr. Z. removed only the two sentinel lymph nodes, rather than doing a full axillary dissection and said to the naked eye, all looked well. Dr. M. performed the first phase of reconstruction. I was able to go home the next day, and while I was in pain from the operation, it was not overwhelming.

Tim made a great nurse administering my meds every four hours with military precision. I couldn't lift my arms very high, so I needed help with everything. I never knew how versatile he could be—he cooked for me, dressed me, and even washed and styled my hair.

On the 18th, the kids arrived tired but happy. What a boost it was to see them! We all began to hope that the worst was over. Then the phone rang. Dr. Z. was calling to break the bad news. Both lymph nodes removed were positive for cancer. He explained what that meant, namely the need for more surgery to check the rest of my lymph nodes, and following that, chemotherapy.

It was strange how calmly we reacted to the news. Our God had prepared all of our hearts. Only three days before I had still been struggling to be at peace with the possibility of metastasis, but God had finally settled that issue in my heart. I'd been on my knees the other evening praying, begging, pleading that God would heal me.

"I know my life is not indispensable, Lord. I can be replaced in every area, in every place—except one—I'm irreplaceable to my kids. Please, please at least let me stay around long enough to get them safely into adulthood."

As I finished that phrase, a thought penetrated my heart, "Yet not as I will, but as You will." I grabbed my Bible and began thumbing through the pages until I got to Matthew, Chapter 26.

"My Father," the Lord cried out, *"if this cannot pass away unless I drink it, Your will be done."* Suddenly, peace flooded my troubled heart. Three times, the Lord Himself had asked that if there was any other way for God to fulfill His plan that Christ might not have to face the agony of the cross. I realized that there was nothing wrong with a heartfelt plea for *"this cup to be removed from me."* Begging wasn't necessary, though. All I needed to do was ask my Father and then trust that He would do what was best.

So, the tears shed after hearing the bad news were not tears of fear but of sadness for my family. This whole ordeal had just got longer and harder on everyone. Tim came into the room and said, "Carole, you're going to be fine, I just know it." Then he proceeded to tell me of an interesting experience he had had the day of my surgery.

"Pastor Steve and I went to lunch, and after returning to the waiting room, I was approached by a woman who asked me if I was here because my wife had cancer. I told her I was. She said, 'I've never done anything like this before, but the Lord told me to come and talk to you. Four years ago, I had cancer in nine organs. Today, I am cancer free. I just wanted to tell you that your wife is going to be fine.'"

I went back into the hospital for more surgery, accompanied by Becky this time as Tim had returned to Japan to work. Becky held my hand and displayed amazing composure for being only fifteen years old. I marveled at the maturity she exhibited as she took on her Daddy's role of nurse over the next few days. Thankfully, no more tumor cells were found in the other six lymph nodes removed.

"That doesn't mean you are cancer free," my oncologist Dr. F. cautioned. "Cancer cells have definitely spread to other parts of your body. The question is how many."

I liked Dr. F., a Texas boy who was not a whole lot bigger than me. "You don't appear to have any other symptoms that would indicate a problem elsewhere, so I feel that we are probably dealing with micro metastasis," he drawled. "However, because of your young age and the amount of time that your tumor went undiagnosed, I'm going to recommend that you have two courses of chemo. It may be a bit of overkill, but I would rather do more than less.

"We want to make sure that the cancer never recurs because if it does, you're in for the fight of your life. I realize you want to get home to Japan as soon as possible, so it is your decision whether you want one or both courses of chemo. Personally, I feel that you should have both, but it's up to you."

I told him I would talk it over with Tim later on, but that I was ready to get started with the first round of chemotherapy. He checked the calendar to see if enough time had elapsed since my latest surgery.

"Physically, you can get started anytime," he said.

"Great, how about tomorrow?"

He did a quick double take, glancing at me as if he wondered whether my real problem was insanity rather than cancer.

"You know, I've never had a patient get this excited about starting chemo before. I'll see you tomorrow."

Tim called later on and I filled him in on my appointment with Dr. F.

"Carole," he said, "you're going to take every last drop of chemo that the doctor wants to give you. Stop worrying about how long this is going to take. You have one thing and one thing only that you are to concern yourself with from now on and that is getting better. I don't want you thinking about anything else."

He wouldn't be back before my first treatment, but reinforcements were standing by. My best friend, Lisa Y., had just flown in from Michigan to provide moral support for the first chemo treatment.

Over the next six months, I would be receiving two different types of chemo. The first round included a harmless looking red liquid called Adriamycin, which was developed by the Japanese during WWII. After seeing the effects of that medicine on my body I heartily pitied the poor little lab rat that had tested that drug out. Taking Adriamycin is a lot like drinking poison.

Each chemo treatment was virtually the same. I'd show up and be greeted with a big hug from Mary Lee who runs the office, the sweetest southern belle you'll ever meet. Then, Michelle, the lab tech, would do a blood draw to check my blood counts. I'd see Dr. F. for a quick exam and then if my blood counts were OK, Cheryl, the nurse oncologist, would give me my treatment. She was so great at her job—compassionate, professional, and funny. She'd join us in prayer and then hook up my IV.

As she started the treatment she'd pause, cupping her hand around her ear, "Listen," she'd say, "Do you hear them? All those nasty little cancer cells are screaming and running for their lives!"

The actual treatment wasn't too bad. The worst part about it was the preliminary dose of steroids that I was given to ward off any allergic reactions. Sixty seconds after the steroids were injected into my IV, instant seasickness would begin followed by the unsettling sensation of being burned from the top to literally your bottom. How I despised that part of the treatment!

To pass the time, we'd read or socialize with the other patients who felt like visiting. Some folks were just too sick or scared or depressed to talk. One guy was a hoot—his chemo hadn't caused hair loss, but he wore a hat anyway—or hats, I should say. He sat across the room from us, absorbed in a magazine, wearing a serious look and an Indian style turban. The next time I happened to glance over, he was wearing a bright red and white striped number that made him look like The Cat in the Hat. Later, he donned a classy beret. The switch was always performed when no one was looking at him, and the funniest part about it was that the guy continued to pore over his magazine with an innocent look as if nothing was going on. This amusing behavior continued for at least an hour, but by then my "cocktail" would be finished and we would head home.

I left after the first treatment feeling almost cocky.

"Hey, this isn't so bad. I don't feel a thing!" I even went home and had lunch … big mistake. The nausea began three hours later as I was sitting in a coffee shop with Lisa. By the time we left there, I was in pretty bad shape.

Chemo drugs kill cancer cells in a couple of different ways. One way they work is by targeting and destroying any cells in the body that are rapidly dividing, like cancer cells. While chemo drugs are very powerful, they are not very smart or discriminating. They not only kill off cancer cells, but also any other cells in the body that divide rapidly, like your skin cells, hair cells, bone marrow cells, and the cells that line your intestinal tract. As a result, there are a myriad of severe side effects. Within hours I was so sick that I became frightened. This lasted for five days—I couldn't keep anything down. Ten days after the first treatment, every hair on my body vacated its post, and I was abruptly plunged into menopause.

Hearing of my discomfort, Dr. F. decided to adjust my dosage for the next treatment. "We're walking a fine line here," he would say. "The trick is to kill the cancer cells without killing you."

I told him I would appreciate that. Subsequent treatments only made me ill for three days after that. My family called it a resurrection—after three days I would weakly crawl out of bed, and Tim and the kids would usher me to the neighborhood IHOP restaurant. There I'd polish off a stack of steaming hot, golden pancakes drowned in a lake of sweet maple syrup followed by a mega-sized veggie omelet.

After that, my bulging stomach and I would head out for a short walk. The legs were still a little unsteady, but my motto was, "If I can still move, that means I'm not dead."

During the first course, my treatments were given about once a month. After a while, my medical team realized that Tim and I were really OK with this whole cancer thing, and everyone loosened up around us. As we would leave the office, Dr. F. would poke his head out of his door and yell, "Come on, stagger and moan will ya? You just had chemo, and you're making me look bad! I've got a reputation to keep up!"

I'd tease back, "You call that chemo? I'm not even puking. Doc, you're slacking off. Better work on it for next time."

Nehemiah 8:10 says, *"The joy of the Lord is my strength."* It was incredible how the Lord kept our spirits up during this time. Most everyone we knew lost their sense of humor when I got sick, but not my family. They teased me unmercifully. It became a huge joke for me to try to get out of doing things that I didn't like.

I'd whine, "Oh, I can't possibly clean the house. After all, I have cancer," to which someone in my family would respond, "Aw, Mom, quit trotting out that old cancer excuse again, will ya?"

Tim would chip in from the other room, "Get out there and start cleaning, and after that you can pull the transmission out of the car!"

It didn't even bother any of us that I was completely bald. I actually thought it was a good look for me, and talk about easy! Just jump out of the shower and buff the scalp with a towel until it shone. I decided against wearing a wig, and instead opted for various hats and scarves—making sure to wear neutral gang colors, of course. It was Phoenix after all. In fact, the rest of the family soon followed suit—wearing hats, scarves, and even buzzing their heads to express their support.

I am sure people began to wonder whether my type of baldness was contagious. It was one thing to see Dan and Tim to shave their heads and quite another for Rachel to follow suit. She did, though, and I thought she was the most beautiful person I'd ever seen. Of the many loving gestures that were extended to me during this time, 14-year-old Rae's was the best.

Tim returned from Japan with great news. He had originally planned to go back and forth between Japan and Phoenix during my treatment in order to keep his job. But, it became pretty obvious after hearing how the treatment had affected me that our family ought to be together during this time.

I practically begged Tim to move us permanently to Phoenix. He approached his bosses at the base in Misawa and offered to resign, but instead of accepting his resignation, they expressed complete support of our family, telling Tim to take whatever time he needed and that his job would be waiting for him when he returned. What an answered prayer!

So, we settled into a semi-furnished condo for the long haul. Gary F. approached us at church the following Sunday and insisted that I give him a list of anything our family could use during our stay in Phoenix. I rattled off a few things, and by the next week, our church family had lent us everything that we needed.

"Nothing unites the individual parts of a body like the pain network," writes Phillip Yancey in his book Where is God When it Hurts?

"I have become aware of the body's vital need to sense pain. Pain is the very mechanism that forces me to stop what I'm doing and pay attention to the hurting member. It makes me stop playing basketball if I sprain an ankle, change my shoes if they're too tight, go to the doctor if my stomach keeps hurting. In short, the healthiest body is the one that feels the pain of its weakest parts ... We—you, I—are part of God's response to the massive suffering in this world. As Christ's body on earth we are compelled to move, as He did, toward those who hurt. In moments of extreme suffering or grief, very often God's love is best perceived through the flesh of ordinary people like you and me. In such a way we can indeed function as the body of Jesus Christ."

Dr. Paul Brand elaborates on this idea, "So much of the sorrow in the world is due to the selfishness of one living organism that simply doesn't care when the next one suffers. In the body, if one cell or group of cells grows and flourishes at the expense of the rest, we call it cancer and know that if it is allowed to spread the body is doomed. And yet, the only alternative to the cancer is absolute loyalty of every cell to the body, the head. God is calling us today to learn from the lower creation ... "

There was never a single moment during cancer treatment where my family questioned the love of God because He made His presence felt and known on a daily basis, not only through His word, but also through His people. So many loving, sacrificial gestures were made that we would remark later on that the ordeal of cancer had been one of the sweetest times of our lives. The body of Christ—our friends, family and even strangers—became the presence of God to us.

7

"No Pain, No Gain"

My parents, who lived in Wyoming, decided to relocate to Phoenix during my treatment. Initially, they took the news of my diagnosis pretty hard, which was understandable considering what had happened to my sister. While still in Japan, Tim had offered to call and break the news to them, but I felt that they should hear it from me. I had only seen or heard my strong, loving father cry four times during my lifetime. My phone call made it five. But, by the time they arrived in Phoenix, their spirits had rebounded and they were in "fight mode." They had both been reading books and talking to doctors about my disease, and they were educated and ready to help. There was something else, too—a new awareness of God.

My family and I had not always seen eye to eye on spiritual matters, and that had caused some tension over the years. But from the moment Mom and Dad walked in our door, we could see that an awakening was taking place. Mom came in beaming and said, "For years you have been telling us about God working in your lives—you called it 'seeing God's fingerprints all over the place. Well, for the first time in our lives, we've seen God's fingerprints."

Then they proceeded to tell us of several significant answers to prayer that they had seen over the past few weeks. Their reaction came as a relief to us. My folks had been a little bitter towards God after my sister passed away, and we feared that the news of my cancer would drive them even further from Him. But, God, in His amazing wisdom, used my battle with cancer to draw my parents closer to Himself, and by the end of the winter, Mom had been transformed by the love of God.

"Oh the depth of the riches both of the wisdom and knowledge of God! How unsearchable are His judgments and unfathomable His ways!" Romans 11:33

November 2002

I am sure there are many, many reasons for this trial in my life. I will probably be allowed to know some of them. Other reasons I will never know. It has been exciting to go deeper into the unfathomable, inexhaustible riches of God's grace. He has been nearer to me than ever before. I am thrilled beyond words at how God has used this in Mom's life. That in itself has made this whole experience worthwhile.

By this time, I should have three chemo treatments behind me. But, alas, although I arrived ready for treatment, my white blood cells did not. I praise God even in this because the week prior, when my white blood cell count would have been at its lowest point making me highly susceptible to life threatening infection, my entire family became ill with terrible head and chest colds and even some sort of stomach virus. I walked in the midst of these harmful germs unscathed. I felt untouchable, as if I had a force field surrounding me! Thank you, Father.

Secondly, the girls and I had purchased tickets to see Beth Moore speak, and had I had chemo on time, I would have been too sick to attend. I was able to go with them and have a marvelous time praising and worshipping God with 3,000 other women. As I looked around at all of the radiantly joyful faces and heard thousands of sweet voices lifting up our awesome God, I felt I had seen a snapshot of heaven.

Beth Moore is a powerful speaker and writer. I remember one thought-provoking statement from one of her Bible studies: "Do we just want the cross without the resurrection? Are we trying to stuff the living, working Christ back into the tomb so He'll just save us, and then let us alone? Or do we want to know the power of His resurrection and the fellowship of sharing in His sufferings?" (Philippians 3:10) Philippians 1:6 says, "He who began a good work in you will carry it on to completion until the day of Christ Jesus. Yet, we wish He'd stop picking on us the moment we're saved and let us be the boss." How unfortunately true.

Three to four weeks seemed to be just enough time to mentally prepare for the next round of chemo. Right after a treatment, I dreaded so much having to face the next one. But by the time the next treatment rolled around, I felt absolutely feisty! Bring it on! Each time I faced a treatment, I armed myself with memorized verses—something to focus on besides how I bad I was feeling.

Lamentations 3:22–23 was one of my favorites: *"The Lord's loving kindnesses indeed never cease, for His compassions never fail. They are new every morning; Great is Your faithfulness."*

I would meditate on the fact that all of God's resources were at my beck and call. His love, His strength, His peace, His compassion, His grace, and His hope and help were unlimited. Today, if I use up all that He had portioned out to me, and tomorrow if I came to the end of my strength, my peace, my hope, my joy—it was not a problem. God would provide all that I needed for that new day out of the riches of His grace without fail.

December 2002

The holidays have come and gone. We spent Thanksgiving with Gary and Phyllis S.—what a neat family. We already feel so close to them since we "share" their daughter Emily. Emily spent seven weeks of her summer vacation with us in Japan and became like part of our family. (Of course, we made her swear before she left Japan not to reveal any of our family secrets, now that she's one of "Us").

Mom and Dad spent a very simple Christmas with us. A four-foot artificial tree and just a few presents. The kids were very understanding. They have always been so grateful and flexible.

I've made it through the first course of chemo and am set to begin nine treatments of Taxol (second round) in January. Come to find out, I am to have weekly treatments. Dr. F. thinks it will be more effective this way and a bit easier on my system. He worries about my weight and my anemia. I haven't missed any more treatments but have come close because of what Doc calls the Jones' blood counts (meaning very low). Often, my treatments end with a shot of Procrit—it helps my body to form red blood cells and perks me up a little bit. I am a bit leery—will I be constantly sick for nine weeks? Help, Lord.

The second course of chemo turned out to be a snap compared to the toxic first round. My stomach was spared, but between the Taxol treatments and the reconstruction process, I was very tired, very sore, and very achy.

The Taxol gave me shooting pains from my ribs on down, and I often looked like a fidgety child trying to sit still. I continued exercising, figuring that if my legs were going to hurt, I might as well give them a good reason.

Dr. F. has been bragging about me. When a new patient asks him what it will be like to have chemo, he says, "Well, I have one patient who jogs every day, plays tennis, and lifts weights."

During my last appointment, Cheryl asked me to speak with one of their new breast cancer patients who was feeling a bit overwhelmed. Josie had an aggressive tumor that went from the size of a pea to the size of a golf ball in three weeks. Life was a whirlwind for her at the moment and her countenance reflected the fear that she was feeling. We forged an immediate bond—a connection that came from fighting the same battle—and my heart went out to her. We talked a little about cancer and chemo and different ways that I tried to cope with the side effects. I told her that exercise helped, a sense of humor, and getting up everyday and putting on make-up and mascara even though I only had three eyelashes left.

But, our conversation dwelt mainly on spiritual matters because external things can only help so much. I shared with her that I could face cancer with peace because of the security of my relationship with God. I had total assurance that no matter what the outcome of the disease, I was loved by God and would spend eternity with Him. The next week I saw Josie again, and she looked absolutely radiant! All of her hair was gone, but she was wearing an attractive scarf, make-up, and a beautiful smile. I asked her what accounted for the change, and she smiled and pointed up to heaven.

Chemotherapy ended the first week of March. It was time to kick back and start recovering. All that remained was my final reconstructive surgery, which would take place in a month once my blood counts returned to normal. During the last several months, Dr. M. had been injecting saline into the temporary implants, gradually stretching out the pectorals to make a place for the final implants. It was a painful process, but worth it. After all, a woman can't really complain when she gets to go down a size in her jeans and up two sizes in her bra. I had remarked to the doctor several weeks ago that my shirts were getting tight. "Just how big are you going to make me?" I asked.

He replied, "That's entirely up to you."

So glad that I asked! I said, "My family is already calling me 'Barbie.' You better stop before they start calling me 'Dolly'!"

Tim retorted, "Hey, don't be so hasty … what's the matter with being a 'Dolly'?"

My hair tried to make a comeback, and by the end of March I had a definite five—o'clock shadow. Tim would miss waking up in the morning, chuckling at what I had donned in the middle of the night to keep my bald head warm. I think his favorite was the Santa hat.

One glorious spring afternoon, Tim and I went jogging together. Exercising together always gave us some private time to talk. Halfway through our run, Tim looked at me with a huge grin and said, "I am so proud of you, Carole! You've raised the bar for cancer patients everywhere. You should be the poster child for cancer. Talk about kicking butt and taking names. I am so proud of you!"

My heart soared as he reached over and squeezed my hand, and I said, "Thanks for telling me every day that I was beautiful and sexy even though I know I looked like a freak. And, thanks for shouldering all the stress so that I would not have to worry about a thing. I couldn't have made it without you.

"Tim, now that this is almost over, I just want to say one thing. I know you didn't want to talk about this before, but I want to say it now—Dr. F. says that he's cured me and that I am not to give him a bad name by getting sick again, but we both know that there is no cure for breast cancer. If my cancer ever returns and I am terminal, just let me go. Don't hook me up to anything and try to keep me around. I want to go home to heaven."

He replied, "Carole, I know that. This world isn't our home, and I'm as homesick as you are—I'm completely healthy, but I feel exactly the same way. I don't ever want to be kept here artificially and I'd be upset if you tried. I'd rather go home, too. Anyway, it doesn't matter because you beat it, baby!"

In April, Dr. M. performed the final phase of reconstruction. He said it was a homerun—it couldn't have gone any better. Walking away with cleavage was some consolation. Even though we needed to hang around for a few more weeks, we started pulling up roots in preparation for our return to Japan. By May 1, we would be home! Back to Japan and back to our lives! Everyone was giddy with excitement.

April 28, 2003

We're going home. Everyone has been so encouraging throughout this experience. I am grateful, but feel as if I am about to burst with encouragement for them! I want to shout, "The Lord is great! He is good, He is sovereign, He is powerful, and He loves us! Praise His mighty name! Don't feel bad for me. This was not an awful experience!" but no one seems to want to hear what I have to say. Perhaps I am just supposed to soak it all up right now for God to wring out later on?

May 2003

We had a great trip home. I think the wanderlust of the parents has been genetically transmitted to the offspring because our whole family loves traveling. We had a stopover in Narita, and I think I slept in the hotel room for thirteen straight hours. I haven't slept like that in months. Once the wheels touched down on the runway in Misawa, I lost my composure and cried. I can't believe it's over. Robb and Merry D., Col. H., and Major R. (Tim's bosses) met us at the airport.

We sat down with the kids the other evening to talk about the last nine months. Now that we are home, the past few months seem like a dream. So, we wanted to sum things up and talk about what God had done in our lives before it all got too hazy. I guess we can all see some growth in our lives and in the life of my Mom, but the consensus seems to be a scratching of our heads and a "What was that really all about?"

For some reason, known only to God right now, it was necessary for us to be plucked up out of our lives and dropped down into the cancer experience. We aren't sure why, but we are sure of one thing. God is God, and we are not. He is perfect and never makes mistakes. He never lost control of our lives for a moment during the past nine months. With this in mind, we'll be content to leave the reasons for all of this in His capable hands.

> God knows, not I, the reason why
> His winds of storm drive through my door;
> I am content to live or die
> Just knowing this, nor knowing more.
> My Father's hand appointing me
> My days and ways, so I am free.
> —Margaret Sangster

8

"Eye of the Storm"

Dusty, our black lab, was better than any alarm clock. At precisely 5:15 every morning she began poking her cold, wet nose under the covers prodding me into wakefulness whether I was agreeable or not.

"Just in case you forgot, it's time for my walk," she seemed to be saying as she whined and sought after me under the sheets. I rubbed my eyes and glanced over at the window and was relieved to see sunshine peeking through the curtains. Good—it had been a terribly rainy summer. Today, we'd finally have dry roads for our walk, and I might even be able to sneak in a bike ride before the kids woke up.

The sun had been up since about 4:30 a.m. and so had Tim. He was already out on the road somewhere, no doubt exploring a new route that he could guide me on this weekend. He enjoyed the solitude of his early morning bike rides during the week, often riding 25 miles before heading in to work.

July 23, 2003, was just another day in our busy lives. Back in Japan for almost three months now, we were pretty amazed at how easily we had picked up where we left off almost a year ago. Life was sweet and seemed perfect once again. Tim was making up for lost time at work, and both of the girls had landed their first summer jobs. Dan spent most days outdoors, rain or shine (with the emphasis on rain), playing with the neighbor boys.

Misawa was a fantastic place to raise the kids—rural and safe with lots of room to run and play and explore. There were green pastures and thick forests nearby, and we rode bikes or jogged on every trail that we discovered. Gazing at the beauty of Misawa always took me back to the simpler days of my childhood as a farmer's daughter and filled me with peace.

My health steadily grew stronger. In fact, I felt that I had been given back the health of a much younger me. I puttered around at home, doing the things that made me happy. I walked, biked, and jogged mile after mile, and the realization that I hadn't felt this good in years made me nearly giddy. I completely planned out the upcoming school year for the kids, played "Mom the taxi," transporting the kids to their various lessons and jobs, and cooked up a storm now that food tasted good again.

Tim had already left for work by the time I got back from walking Dusty, but I would see him later in the morning when I dropped Becky off at his office. Becky's summer job was at the Health and Wellness Center, working for Tim's boss, Major Jim R. Tim enjoyed having her around and came home everyday beaming with pride over her job performance.

Wednesdays always seemed to be the busiest day of the week for all of us. In addition to work, there were also music lessons in the afternoon, martial arts classes all evening long, and a mid-week church service to attend. As Tim and I shuttled offspring here and there, we'd often touch base for a few minutes. A brief phone call, an e-mail, or quick stop by the office was just enough time for a quick kiss and a "Hang in there, Baby."

That afternoon, as I picked up the girls from work, Tim strolled out to the van for one of our rendezvous. I could tell by the way he was walking that, as usual, he had something amusing to say, and I was already laughing by the time he got to the van. As he neared my rolled down window, he squinted up at the sun and said meekly, "Help! What is that? I'm scared!" alluding to our gloomy, overcast summer weather thus far.

The kids and I played along and laughingly said, "That would be the sun, Daddy. We know you haven't seen it in a while, but it's OK. It won't hurt you."

We joked around for a few more minutes and then Tim said, "So, I'm picking up the girls from voice lessons after work, right?"

"Right," I said, "And I'll drop Daniel off at Tang Soo Do class. Dinner will be ready when you get home."

"OK," he said. "Hey, I found another beautiful route to take you on Saturday morning," referring to our early morning weekend bike rides together. "It's about a 20-miler with a pretty good hill or two. You up for it?"

"No problem. Remember, I'm 'Amazon Mom!'" Astonished by my amazing rebound from cancer treatment, my family had recently given me that nickname.

After stealing a kiss, I said, "See you later," and as I drove away, I thought what a great team we made, how the worst was over now. It was a peaceful, gorgeous, sunny day, and we felt on top of the world.

The cancer experience would never be forgotten, of course. Monthly check-ups would ever be a reminder of that tough time, but we were beginning to view that 10-month period as merely a rough spot on the road of life. Oh sure, it had caused Tim and I to spend lots of time re-evaluating and discussing our priorities and plans during our long bike rides, but we truly felt that the storm had passed and that we were in the clear.

As I mentioned before, my family weathered many typhoons while living on the island of Guam. One fall in particular, we experienced a terrible typhoon season. Six storms passed over our small island in six consecutive weeks. I gave birth to Daniel as one of these storms, Typhoon Brian, landed on the shores of Guam.

The worst storm of this particular stretch was Typhoon Omar. Packing sustained winds of one-hundred-fifty miles per hour with gusts well over one-hundred-eighty miles per hour, it wreaked havoc with much of the island. Homes were destroyed, cars tossed about like children's toys, power lines downed, and valuable water reservoirs were contaminated. We were without electricity and water in our apartment building for nearly a month after that storm. Not fun.

Our apartment building housed twenty-one family units, and during the height of this particular storm, nineteen of those apartments sustained terrific damage as patio doors and windows exploded, reacting to the ferocious winds and pressure fluctuations. Furniture, clothing, and household items were picked up and either strewn across the landscape or hurled through neighbor's adjoining windows.

Interestingly enough, the two units that were not affected at all by this storm housed the only two families in the entire building who confessed Christ as Savior—and who were on their knees praying during the twelve-hour ordeal! The storm became another opportunity to minister to our neighbors as our little home became one of the only refuges from the damaging and frightening winds.

Typhoons are very interesting phenomena. The winds travel in one direction as the first part of the storm passes, and then switch direction once the eye has passed. It's also interesting to note that the winds during the second half of the storm can be even more severe than the first half.

Having lost power in the early hours of Typhoon Omar, we sat for hours by the light of flashlights and candles, listening to the winds howl and cry. Then, suddenly, everything began to quiet down. The raging winds stopped, the driving rain ceased, and the sun tried to make a comeback through the overcast sky.

The children began skipping around clapping their hands shouting, "It's over, it's over! Can we go outside and play now?"

For several minutes, peace prevailed. But, the storm wasn't over. We were in the eye, the dead center, and soon enough the furious winds would return with even greater force, inflicting more damage on the already battered island.

We, too, skipped through this calm period of our lives like little happy children, blissfully unaware that the eye of the storm was nearly past. As we retired the evening of the twenty-third, we had no idea that life as we knew it was over, and that we were about to face the most difficult challenge of our lives.

For years, our family's nightly routine has been to spend a few minutes praying together, often reading the Bible if time allows, and then hugging and kissing each other before heading off to bed. It has always been a Walton-like moment to see the kids trundle off to bed calling out, "I love you, Mommy. I love you, Daddy. You're the best parents ever!"

We call back, "I love you, too," and then turn to each other and say, "And I love you, too."

No unresolved issues, arguments, or problems; nothing left unsaid; no regrets. It always seemed like the right and perfect way to end each day and I'm truly grateful that was my family's habitual practice.

After all, tomorrow is not a guarantee.

9

"Shattered"

○ ○

I will not doubt, though all my ships at sea
Come drifting home with broken masts and sails;
I shall believe the hand that never fails,
From seeming evil worketh good to me.
And, though I weep because those sails are battered
Still will I cry, while my best hopes lie shattered,
I trust in Thee.

—Ella Wheeler Cox

I woke early to find the sleepy village of Misawa engulfed once again in sea fog. Dusty, undeterred by this phenomenon, was raring to go. Most likely the sun would start burning off the fog by the time we were partway into our walk.

Sure enough, 30 minutes down the road, the sun peeked through the clouds. Two days in a row of great weather. "July 24th … about time summer arrived," I muttered to myself.

Dusty, who had been plodding along placidly, suddenly became extremely agitated. She began pulling on her leash, barking, and carrying on.

"What's wrong with you, Dusty? Sit! Stop acting so goofy." Then I heard it. The faint singsong wail of a siren began drawing steadily nearer. I turned around and saw the base ambulance, red cross emblazoned on its camouflaged side, making its way down the highway followed by a Japanese police car. No wonder Dusty was upset. It looked as if the ambulance was heading for the toll road, which meant someone on base was sick or hurt enough to require care at the larger hospital in Hachinohe.

As the ambulance drove by, I automatically started praying for Tim. It's not that I was worried about him, but whenever I hear a siren and someone in my family is out and about, I always stop and pray for their safety and well being. It's one of my personal quirks.

When I returned home, the first thing I noticed was Becky sitting in her dad's chair eating breakfast at the kitchen table instead of Tim. "Did your dad leave for work already?" I inquired.

"I don't know, Mom. I haven't seen him this morning."

"You mean he's not home from his bike ride yet? That's odd. He should be home by now."

A feeling of déjà vu suddenly struck me. I had experienced this exact same moment only a week ago. I'd come home from exercising to find that Tim hadn't returned from his bike ride. After scouting around the house, I noticed that our van was missing from the garage. A few minutes later, Tim had returned to the house, explaining that he'd gotten a flat tire.

"I would have called you to come and get me, but I had no idea how to tell you where I was, Carole. I didn't even know where I was! So, I walked to a gas station and called a cab. Then, when I got home I drove the van back to the station to get my bike. What a hassle. From now on, I'm going to carry an extra inner tube in case I get another flat tire."

"He's got a spare, so it couldn't be another flat tire," I thought to myself as I checked the garage, hoping that Tim's car was gone, indicating that he had left for work earlier than usual. No, it was still there. I walked through the house checking all the rooms.

Finally, I stood helplessly in the kitchen and said to Becky, "I don't know what to do. I don't have any idea where Dad rode his bike this morning. He could be anywhere."

Then, I remembered the ambulance that I'd seen an hour or so earlier. Surely that had nothing to do with Tim. Not knowing what else to do, I picked up the phone and dialed the base emergency room.

"Hello. My name is Carole Jones and my husband Tim works for the HAWC (Health and Wellness Center). He went out for a bicycle ride this morning, and he should be home by now. I have no idea where he rode this morning and I didn't know where else to call, but I happened to see an ambulance this morning around the time he was out riding. I just thought I would check to make sure that a bicyclist wasn't brought into the ER this morning."

The troop on the line paused and said, "Ma'am, could you hold the line, please?" Fear began to grip me, and my stomach started churning. "Please, God, this cannot be happening …"

A few seconds later, a colonel came on the line and introduced himself. Then he asked me if I knew where Tim was. I repeated what I had said before to the young man on the line. The colonel said, "Carole, a bicyclist was brought into the ER a while ago. Can you describe what Tim was wearing?"

There are some people who seem to be able to remember every dream they have ever had. Tim's like that. He wakes up nearly every morning and recounts dream after dream to me in vivid detail. Sometimes, he even experiences recurring dreams.

I, on the other hand, can never seem to remember my dreams. So from this point on, I will not be able to tell you exactly what happened because life had once again taken on a surreal, dream-like quality. My mind immediately began trying to deny the nightmarish reality that it had entered.

"This isn't real. This isn't happening. This is a dream, or somebody else's life," my frightened psyche reasoned. I look back on that day and can only remember disjointed bits and fragments.

Fighting panic, I described what Tim was wearing only to be told that the cyclist brought in had indeed been Tim. I knew immediately that he had to be hurt quite badly. Tim worked daily with the folks at the hospital, and for no one to recognize him was a very bad sign. I was so afraid that this man was going to tell me that Tim was dead.

I remember asking if Tim was OK and asking where he was. The colonel's answers were measured and careful. He was trying to be as honest as he could be without greatly alarming me. He told me that Tim was alive but that he had very serious injuries and had been transported to Hachinohe City Hospital.

The trauma unit at the base hospital was not set up to handle the extensive care that Tim now required. I asked for directions on how to get to the hospital and was asked to remain at my home. Several people that worked with Tim were on their way to our house at this very moment, and they would take us there. The colonel wanted me to remain on the line until the folks from base arrived, but by this time I had turned around to find all three of the kids standing in the living room staring at me, tears streaming down their faces.

"I need to get the kids ready to go and make some phone calls," I said tremulously.

The kids and I stood in the living room for a few minutes with our arms around each other praying for Daddy. I remember telling them that Daddy was hurt, but that he was alive. We clung to that little bit of positive news, comforting each other with, "Everything is going to be OK. God knows exactly where Daddy is right now, and He's with him, taking care of him."

I sent them off to their rooms to get ready to go to the hospital and called Merry D. to ask her to pray. She promised to meet us at the hospital. I quickly fired off an e-mail to everyone in our address book, asking for prayer. I changed out of my sweats. I tried to get the kids to eat something, but no one felt hungry. I made sure the dog was taken out. I put on my coat. I donned my baseball cap to cover up the scant bit of hair that had begun to grow. I picked up my purse. I opened the door to our foyer. Then I paced restlessly. It seemed that as long as I was doing something, as long as I was moving and not thinking, I was all right.

Dietrich Bonhoeffer once said, *"From the very moment one feels called to act is born the strength to bear whatever horror one will feel or see. In some inexplicable way, terror loses its overwhelming power when it becomes a task that must be faced."*

I mention this because that is the only reason that I can come up with to explain how I got through the next few minutes without completely falling apart. I just kept moving, like a robot, taking care of things, going through the motions.

Minutes later, a vehicle pulled up to our house. Out stepped four men in uniform with very somber faces. One of the men, Scott G., I recognized as a troop that Tim worked with at the HAWC. Another man had a cross on his lapel, and I surmised that he was a chaplain from the base. The other men were colonels whom I knew by name, but not by face. Tim had mentioned these men from time to time, but I had never actually met them. As a group, they quietly walked towards our front door.

"Hey, wait a minute," I thought to myself, "this is unbelievable! I've seen this exact scene before. This is the part in the old war movies where the wife is told that her husband's plane has been shot down (or his ship has been sunk, or his tank blown up) and he has been killed. They're coming to tell me that Tim is dead!"

I resolved not to listen to them and determinedly strode out the front door. "Come on, kids, let's go." Panicked that if I slowed down I would hear the worst, I said quickly to the gentlemen at my door, "We're all ready to go. Please take us to the hospital now. Please, if you'll just take us to Tim ..."

One of the officers, Colonel B., stopped me gently but firmly in my tracks by placing his hands on my shoulders. He slowly turned me around and said softly, "Carole, let's go back into the house for a few minutes."

With those words, my composure, as well as my resolve, completely melted away, dissolving in the tears that began streaming down my face.

I was led into the house and made to sit in our rocking chair. Colonel B. never let go of me for a minute. I managed to choke out between sobs, "Did … T.. Tim … is … is … he … alive?"

Gravely, we were told about the accident and Tim's condition. He was in bad shape—really bad shape. He was in a coma and he was alive, but they didn't know if he would make it or not.

With each word, I saw the kids fearfully retreat across the living room to their dad's recliner. They huddled together, hugging each other, and crying softly. I think I was being held down in the chair, I don't really remember. But, I struggled to my feet and staggered over to join the kids in their dad's chair. This moment was the first of many to follow where I felt completely incompetent to help our children.

I pulled all three kids into my lap, and not knowing what else to do for them, I prayed. The chaplain, upon hearing me pray, crossed the living room and put his arms around all of us and added his prayers to mine.

We sat there for a long time. I kept asking the men to take us to Tim, but they said we needed to wait for word from the hospital. They said they were waiting to hear that Tim had arrived and was stabilized. I'd seen the ambulance over two hours ago, and I felt sure that Tim was at the hospital by now. I wondered if Tim's condition was so critical that his death was imminent and that the men were expecting that word at any moment.

I didn't like waiting, kept thinking that my place was with Tim. Having to sit and do nothing was excruciatingly painful.

Finally, word came and we set off for the hospital, which was 45 minutes away. I think Col. B. drove our van and that a translator accompanied us from the base.

No one said much as we drove to the hospital. Words weren't necessary, though, because I could read the expressions on our children's faces. Fear. They were terrified and so was I. I think we read a Psalm and prayed together. Daniel was copying verses from his Bible onto a piece of paper. He looked over at me and said, "Hey, Mommy? Did you see Scott G.? He was crying."

Tim had been working with Daniel, now 10 years old, trying to teach him not to cry so easily over little things. When I protested, Tim had said, "He's getting to be a big boy now and he needs to toughen up." Hmm …

I said, "Yes, I saw him Danny. I think he just loves your dad so much and feels really badly about what has happened. It's OK for a man to cry when he's feeling really bad. Even your daddy cried when your Grandpa Bob died."

"He did?"

"He sure did."

Then Dan, who must've heard his dad say numerous times, "It takes a lot to make a grown man cry," said quietly, "Yeah, it takes a grown man to cry, Mommy."

I glanced over at the girls. They stared numbly out the windows of the van, their eyes merely pretending to take in the Japanese countryside. I'd manage to pull myself together for a few seconds, but then a torrent of fresh tears would be released as those awful words intruded into my thoughts again and again: "We don't think he's going to make it …"

10

"Prognosis"

July 24, 2003
Dear Family and Friends,

My heart is breaking as I write this to you—this morning Tim was struck by a car. He is in a coma and has a very serious brain injury, as well as other injuries.

We are still greatly indebted to you all for your love and prayer support during my cancer treatment, but I know that I can ask you again for your prayers.

I cannot give you a prognosis—everything that I have been told has been pretty negative. We need a miracle.

Carole

Driving through a city that we had never visited before, pulling up to a strange hospital in a foreign country, walking past strangers whose language we couldn't understand, and glancing at signs that we were unable to comprehend only added to the unreal feeling of the situation.

We were grateful to be met and embraced by Robb and Merry D. and their daughter, Melody. They are all so fabulous, positive, and strong that I was surprised to see Melody and Merry on the verge of tears. Their reaction and the concern on their faces penetrated my foggy mind, and I remembered thinking, "Tim must be really, really, really bad!"

Robb D., usually very upbeat, looked like he felt sick. I found out later that one of the nurses at the hospital who was a mutual friend was the first to recognize Tim in the base emergency room. Knowing that we were close friends of Robb and Merry, he had gone to Robb, one of the orthopedic PAs and said, "You know the biker who was brought in a while ago? I think it's Tim Jones."

Robb was so stunned, and he said he just sat there for several moments wondering how in the world he was going to tell me the horrible news. I guess at that very moment, I called the ER.

Stacey S., who had been my surgeon, was there, too, and she walked up and gave me a hug. I hadn't seen her since we got back to Japan, and I think she asked me how I was doing since the cancer.

I wanted to be taken immediately to Tim, but again, they made me wait for a while. I let myself be led around ... sit here ... wait over there. I think that a couple of Japanese policemen asked me a few questions. I don't even remember what we talked about, but I'll never forget the looks on their faces as they said, "We're so sorry about your husband."

Abject pity. They felt so sorry for us. It was a look that I would become more than accustomed to over the next few months.

For hours, I'd been walking as if in a dream. My mind kept trying to reject the gravity of Tim's condition. After all, he'd always been there for me and the kids, and I couldn't even imagine an existence that didn't include him. He'd always been so healthy and strong, so I couldn't wrap my mind around any other mental image of him. Not until I walked into the emergency room and got my first glimpse of his broken body did the awful truth begin to sink in.

I remember walking into the ER and seeing a bunch of people milling around on one side of the room. They were watching me. My eyes began to pan around the room, and I saw a man lying on a bloodstained gurney. His face, particularly the right side, was cut and scraped and bloody. Blood was draining out of one of his ears. Both eyes were grotesquely swollen shut, and my first fleeting thought was, "That doesn't even look like Tim. Maybe there's been a mistake ..." But then I noticed the new red bike shirt, and the black bike shorts that we'd just bought for Tim, and the goatee he had recently begun to sport.

"Oh, no ... no, Tim!" I whimpered feebly. He was nearly unrecognizable. Bits of glass from the windshield of the van were still imbedded in his face. Part of his mustache was scraped off. He was motionless, except for the steady rise and fall of his chest.

He didn't act as if he was in any pain, but nearly every limb was bruised, cut and swollen. The pain would have been horrific had he been conscious, and I remember thinking it was a blessing that he wasn't awake.

If sheer desire and will could alter the events of our lives, the nightmare that we had been forced to enter would have ended immediately, because I stood there praying, wanting, wishing, and willing with all my might for time to reverse, for the accident to have never happened, for things to return to the way they were only hours ago. If only wishing could make it so ...

By the time I reached the side of the gurney, I was shaking so badly that I could hardly stand. Tim was so hurt and mangled everywhere, and I stood uncertainly beside him, wanting to reach out and touch him. I wanted to gather him into my arms and to hold him as tight as I could, but I kept drawing back in fear. I was afraid to touch him, afraid that I would cause him more pain. I finally lightly touched and kissed his forearm, the only spot that wasn't covered in blood, and whispered, "Tim, I'm here. I'm finally here, baby. I'm so sorry you're hurt, but it's going to be OK."

After a few minutes, I was taken out of the ER so that Tim could be moved upstairs to the intensive care unit. Meanwhile, Merry helped me to find a phone so that I could make calls to our family and friends in the states. I remember slumping down into a little pile on the floor as I told Kay, Tim's mom, what had happened.

It was several hours before we were able to see Tim again, and by this time several of our friends had arrived at the hospital to keep us company. The hospital was amazingly accommodating as far as letting people see Tim in intensive care.

Tim looked so awful—he was breathing on his own, but being assisted by a ventilator and was still such a bloody mess that I debated whether to let our kids see him or not. But, finally, I took Becky and Rachel into his room. I held off taking Daniel back to Tim's bedside because I thought it would be too disturbing and upsetting, but when the girls and I headed into the intensive care unit Daniel must have become inconsolable. Someone led him back to us, and the four of us sat by Tim's side and cried.

I think I encouraged the kids to talk to Tim, which triggered numerous questions. Is Daddy going to be OK? Can he hear us? What's wrong with him? I couldn't really answer their questions because I didn't know that much myself, so we just sat there in shock and disbelief watching his chest rhythmically rise and fall. Before the kids returned to the lobby, we prayed together, and they told their daddy they loved him. I wondered if they were seeing their dad for the last time.

Some time later, we had our first meeting with Dr. O., the neurosurgeon assigned to Tim's case. I remember that in every meeting that I had with the Japanese neurosurgeons I was accompanied by one or more of the doctors from the base and sometimes a translator although the Japanese doctor spoke English pretty well.

I was extremely grateful for their presence because I was completely ignorant as far as what questions I should ask the doctor, what treatment to expect for Tim, and their expertise and wisdom was greatly appreciated. I also remember that every single meeting with the doctors was like receiving a physical beating. As test results came in and treatment progressed, the news kept getting bleaker and bleaker, and I would walk away from those meetings most often in tears and in need of strong arms to hold me up.

You've heard the expression, "adding insult to injury"? That's a perfect description of the progress of a traumatic brain injury. Tim was struck mainly on the right side of his body and head causing the first serious damage to occur. The momentum from being struck on the head caused his brain to shift inside the cranium, and as it struck the inside of the bony box that was originally designed by God to protect us, the other side of his brain was injured as well

Damaged brain tissue begins to bleed and swell. There's nowhere for the excessive fluid to go inside the cranium, and the pressure that builds up ends up causing as much or more damage to the brain tissue than the original insult. For this reason, Dr. O. was against doing any kind of surgery on Tim. The intracranial pressure was already increasing rapidly and surgery would only exacerbate that. Plus, he said, the two hematomas Tim had would not really benefit from surgery. So, he suggested a treatment that I have since learned is a bit experimental in the states—hypothermia and Mannitol.

After a brain injury, the brain begins producing certain chemicals that are harmful to the injured tissues. Moderate hypothermia—also called body cooling—is thought to slow or prevent the production of these chemicals. As brain swelling increases, the precious oxygen required by the brain is restricted, furthering damage. Hypothermia decreases the amount of oxygen needed by the brain, providing some protection during this critical period. Induced hypothermia is also thought to slow the body's metabolic processes, which otherwise aggravate the injury. It can also help control brain swelling. Mannitol, used in conjunction with this treatment, is a drug used to help flush excessive fluids from the body.

It was pretty obvious that Dr. O. didn't think that there was much to be done for Tim, but I was all for trying anything and everything. Dr. Stacey S. argued for a shunt to be placed in Tim's brain to help drain off the fluid, but again, Dr. O. said no surgery. They eventually compromised and placed a monitor in Tim's brain so that the amount of intracranial pressure could at least be measured. I remember sitting for hours completely engrossed in watching the readouts from the various monitors. Heart rate, blood pressure, intracranial pressure, temperature, oxygenation of the blood—each little variation in his vital signs causing my own heart to race.

Tim had several other injuries: fractured skull, fractured bones in his right hand, fractured right ankle and leg, and fractured ribs on the right side. He was also bleeding internally in his chest. And while all of these injuries were severe, Tim's brain injury made all else pale in comparison.

Some people don't like to know any more than they need to know in difficult circumstances. Ignorance is bliss. But, I am just the opposite. The unknown makes me more fearful than hearing the nitty gritty truth. So, I point blank asked the doctor, "I realize that you're not God (I might have offended the man on that point!), but in your opinion, what are Tim's chances?"

Over the next few weeks, I learned a thing or two about the Japanese culture. First off, Japanese doctors don't like to talk to the primary people involved in a case, especially if they have to give bad news. Usually, they tell someone a bit removed from the center and then let the news filter through family members. As a result, the doctor was a little put off and uncomfortable having to talk directly to me. I tried to respect his culture, but it was very frustrating and difficult. This was my husband, and I wanted to know what was going on!

Dr. O. showed me CT scans of Tim's brain, pointing out the damage. He indicated the two "bleeds"—one on the right near Tim's ear and the other on the front left. The area around the brain was diminished because of swelling, and the accumulating pressure had caused the brain to shift off-center. He referred to Tim's EEG (measures brain activity) which was abnormally slow, and the depressing results from a couple of other tests.

Then he said during the next few hours as the brain swelling increased Tim had a 50/50 chance of experiencing brain death and dying. Even if he survived this first critical period, he would be severely disabled. He predicted that Tim would go into a vegetative state.

I had no idea what he was talking about, so he explained that it meant that Tim would be bedridden, unable to communicate, and need to be fed through a feeding tube. I pictured in my mind someone who had suffered a debilitating stroke, who needed help moving, feeding, and caring for himself, but who at least knew the people around them and eventually got better. Boy, was I mistaken.

The nurses cleaned and stitched Tim up as best as they could. Treatment was started, and Tim's body was packed all over in ice bags. The ice effectively lowered his body temperature, but care had to be taken so that the ice itself didn't touch him because it caused his skin to blister. As his body temperature dropped, Tim would shiver and shake—that was the only movement that we saw from him.

The doctors and nurses would try to elicit responses from Tim by digging a knuckle into his sternum or by tightly pinching his fingernails, arms, or shoulders. They'd talk loudly and inflict pain to get him to react. Tim would merely hunch his shoulders forward with his arms and fists turning inward each time this was done. The doctors told me that they could judge from Tim's response how serious the injury was and what parts of the brain were affected.

Simply put, you have a higher part of your brain and a lower part. The higher part of our brain basically makes us who we are. Our memories, actions, thoughts, ability to communicate, learn, talk, walk, reason, etc., are all controlled by this higher portion of the brain. The lower you go into the brain, the more basic the responses get. These responses from Tim, called posturing, are abnormal, very basic responses from the lowest part of the brain (and brain stem) and indicated that the higher portions of Tim's brain were damaged.

July 26, 2003

Dear Family and Friends,

Thank you so much for your prayers. The kids and I feel them. It is well with our soul. Tim's condition is basically unchanged.

The swelling in his brain has slightly decreased. The treatment being used (hypothermia) can only be used for three days, so starting tomorrow (Sunday our time), the re-warming process will begin. It takes a few days to complete, and the bleeding and swelling could begin again. We won't really know whether the treatment was effective until Tim is warmed up again and tests are repeated.

Tomorrow is critical, so please pray. I realized that I did not tell you that Tim was on his bicycle when he was hit. The van that struck Tim was driven by a 58-year-old Japanese woman who was on her way to the mountains to visit a medium (someone who contacts the dead). Interesting. She is unhurt, but please pray for her. Her van was totaled. I've been told that the front of her van looks as if it struck a telephone pole.

To the Misawa Community:

Thank you, thank you, thank you from the bottom of our hearts for everything you have done for us. Words cannot express our love and gratitude.

Seems to me I remember reading of another resurrection taking place on the third day. We pray that Tim's will start tomorrow.

In His Grip,

Carole and Kids

11

"Watching and Waiting"

Watching and waiting—the new routine. I stayed at the hospital with Tim, and the kids (and dog) went home each day with Robb and Merry. I would sit with Tim as late in the evening as I was allowed and then retire to the "family room"—a Japanese-style sleeping room with an adjoining bathroom and kitchenette area. I'd get up at 6:30 a.m., take a bath as best I could in the sink, change into the fresh clothes that Merry would bring me each day, and be ready and waiting at 7 a.m. when visiting hours started. I'd take off my shoes, put on the plastic slippers provided by the hospital, and wash my hands in disinfectant. Then, I'd sit with Tim, talk to him, read to him, often being kept company by the kids and our friends.

People prayed constantly over Tim and sang to him. Every couple of hours, we'd be kicked out of the ICU so that they could work on Tim in some way. His lungs had to be suctioned, diapers changed, blood drawn, and tests run. During those hours, we'd sit in the lobby and visit with everyone.

For the first three days, the kids and I cried and cried and cried. Then, the tears stopped. This troubled Becky, Rae, and Dan. They felt sort of guilty for not crying anymore and thought that people might think they didn't care about their dad.

Rubbish. I told them that I thought that it was our mind's way of dealing with the grief that we were experiencing. It was trying to protect us by putting us into a numb state where we couldn't constantly feel the pain of our circumstances. I said, too, "It must be normal because it happened to all of us at the exact same time. Plus, we know that thousands of people are praying for us. I think we're feeling those prayers."

Over the next year and a half, the children and I would walk a difficult road together experiencing myriad emotions. If I did one thing for the kids during this entire time, it was to make them feel normal. Each time they shared a struggle with me about some thought they'd had or some feeling they were experiencing, I could say, "Been there, done that already. You are not alone."

At the hospital, I was rarely alone, too. Our church family from Calvary Baptist Church where we had just recently become members, the Misawa community, Tim's co-workers, and our church family from the base chapel brought us meals, sat with us, prayed with us, and made sure that the kids were brought to the hospital each day. Sometimes, different ones would spend the entire night with me. Some of these people were basically strangers to us before Tim's accident, but soon we were as close as family.

One couple from Calvary, Mark and Michiko B., stopped by and offered to translate for us. Their son, Shuhei, had hydrocephalus and had been treated for years by the same neurosurgeons who were now treating Tim. They were familiar with the hospital, the staff, the terminology … what a godsend. Plus, we hit it off immediately.

Tim's accident devastated the entire base community, and everybody rallied in support of our family. The day before Tim's accident, a young airman had been killed while riding his motorcycle and the base was still reeling from that tragedy. So much food was brought to Robb and Merry's home that the neighbor's refrigerators had to be commandeered. Gifts poured in. We were overwhelmed by the generosity and goodness shown to us.

When Tim originally began working for the military on Guam, it was as the base athletic director. But over the years, he'd picked up various classes and courses until he was qualified to become a fitness program manager. His job was basically to keep the troops "fit to fly," and it was also unique in that he eventually seemed to meet everyone on the base. Many, many people kept stopping by or writing notes telling me what an impact Tim had had on them in some way. As we'd meet new people, they'd ask about our family and often want more explanation about the beliefs we kept talking about.

Eventually, the girls took turns staying the night with me at the hospital. We'd sit with Tim until 9 or 10 at night and then walk laps around the gigantic lobby for over an hour, play games, or watch movies. I was having a difficult time sleeping, so I had to basically wear myself out before lying down at night if I had any hope of catching a few winks.

Daniel was getting restless being at the hospital every day. We invented things to keep him occupied. One thoughtful friend, Tina J., who knew that I was normally a very active person, had brought me a bunch of rubber tubing so that I could exercise. We'd take the tubing and tie Daniel up with several of them, and then time him to see how long it took him to get loose. He loved it, and so did passersby. It was highly entertaining, and we found out that the kid was a regular Houdini. We'd play catch in the hallways, play games, and Don W., our missionary friend, brought the kids bags of yen for the concession machines.

You know, you can get most anything from a vending machine in Japan ... eggs, beer, hot coffee or soup, sweets, sodas, ice cream, and even vitamin drinks. Eventually, Tina and her family offered to take Daniel on day trips to get him away from the hospital for a while.

Becky went home each day and printed out the e-mails that came pouring in from family and friends. She also sent out e-mails for me as I was basically still living at the hospital. Up to this point, no one had yet said, "Tim's not going to die," and I wasn't going to leave his side until I knew for sure that he was out of danger. It was Becky who eventually came up with the idea of a Web site as a means of keeping in touch with stateside folks.

July 27, 2003

Dear Family and Friends,

Yesterday morning, I forgot to tell you that there had been a mild earthquake while I was sitting and reading the Bible to Tim. I told him that it was probably the Lord Himself coming down to Japan to see for Himself what the outcry about Tim Jones was all about ... thanks to your fervent prayers.

Today (Sunday), they were supposed to start warming Tim, but they decided that they would keep him in this hypothermic state for one more day. This is not usually done because at about three days, the risks to the rest of the body really begin to outweigh the benefits of the treatment. Tim has kept himself so fit and strong, though, that his body and vital signs have remained very stable, very good.

Other than that, nothing much has changed. The pressure in his cranium is getting lower—that is good. So Monday, our time, they will begin to warm Tim back up.

Today as we were leaving ICU, one of the Japanese male nurses approached us to ask what we were singing about as we sat with Tim. He said the songs were very beautiful. We told him, through our translator, that our songs were about our mighty God and that we were praising Him. He has also been fascinated by the many friends who have come to pray over Tim. Please pray that this man will accept a Japanese New Testament.

It was apparent from the beginning that the faith of my family was on display not only with the Japanese people but with the base community as well. Friends started reporting to me that people were wondering at the strength and peace we exhibited, and that that had led to several opportunities to share the Gospel. Even though it was hard to be glad about anything at the moment, this news was thrilling. God began to work mightily in so many lives, and I knew that Tim would say that whatever the cost, it was worth it.

Over the next several days, Tim's body temperature was gradually returned to normal. Slowly, the amount of sedation that he was being given was reduced so that the doctors could evaluate his neurological condition.

August 6, 2003

Dear Family and Friends,

I was finally able to meet with Tim's doctor today. Wonderful folks from the Med group were there, as well, to make sure that all my questions were answered, and that I understood everything that was discussed.

Here's the gist of it: The swelling in Tim's brain seems to have decreased a bit more, but it appears that the increased pressure caused further damage to his brain stem as well as areas in his higher brain. That's what we were afraid of.

As his sedation level was decreased, several neurological studies were done. These studies, coupled with the latest images in his CT scan, led the doctor to believe that there was, indeed, serious, permanent damage to Tim's brain. Yet, Tim is breathing spontaneously (he's still on the ventilator, but it's just assisting his breathing) and his heart is beating. He isn't considered brain dead, yet he remains comatose. We have seen some movement since they have reduced his level of sedation and taken him off the muscle paralyzer. The doctors say that his movements are only reflexive. However, we have seen some movements that we believe were in response to our touch and voice.

The doctor at this point really doesn't know whether Tim will recover or not. Only God knows that, and HE is the one who will have the final say. Our hope is in Him.

At any rate, we will be heading back to the States very soon. Since we don't know how long Tim's recovery will take, this will probably be a permanent move for us.

I hope that no one thinks that God hasn't been listening just because Tim isn't up and around yet. God has heard every prayer, and just because we don't get exactly the answer we want when we want it doesn't make Him any less God. He is good, He is sovereign, He loves us, and He knows what He's doing. These circumstances don't change His character. We're not throwing in the towel just yet—we're still praying for a miracle.

Please pray for the kids. They've been great throughout all of this. Continue to pray for their strength, especially since we'll be moving—again.

I've been at the hospital for two weeks. Thank you so much for the overwhelming support you have given us. Thank you for writing, calling, visiting with my family, for coming by the hospital to pray for Tim, for translating, for driving my family, for spending the night with the girls and me, for entertaining Daniel, for arranging meals and transportation, for all the food, water, Yen, books, music, etc. you've brought. Thanks, Misawa, what an awesome community. We're sad to leave. Robb and Merry and family—we love you!

Love,

Carole and Kids

Each time we met with the doctors, my hopes and dreams of a recovery for Tim would be shattered. But then, someone would tell me another story of a friend of a friend who'd made a miraculous recovery from a brain injury, or give me a book detailing someone's comeback, and I would rebound. I clung to those encouraging stories as well as the Gospel accounts of Christ healing the blind, sick, and lame. I knew a God who could do anything! My God could raise the dead! How hard could it be to fix a few brain cells? I guess the real question wasn't "Can God heal Tim?" but "Would He?"

Luke 8: 50 Hearing this, Jesus said to Jairus, "Don't be afraid; just believe, and she will be healed."

12

"Roles Reversed"

August 6th, our 20th wedding anniversary, came and went without fanfare. The day, for me, was marked with great confusion. Instead of holing up in a little cabin in the woods with my lover like we'd planned, I was sitting next to him, praying that he would live just one minute more.

I kept asking the Lord, "What was the past 20 years for? Didn't I thank you every single day for my husband and my family? I don't need something like this to make me appreciate what I had! I knew that I was blessed, and I was so grateful! We sacrificed and made our family a priority because we thought that's what You wanted. Didn't I ask you every single day to keep us together and to protect us? There are too many broken families out there in the world. How can one more possibly help?"

Tim's words when I was diagnosed with cancer kept coming back to me, "Carole, I think this is a spiritual attack." At the time, I hadn't thought so, but now it was clear to me that we were in somebody's sights.

Around this time, the base was experiencing one of their many exercises. These exercises came up periodically and were supposed to simulate the "real thing"—possible conflict with an enemy. These were tiring, very strenuous times for the troops, but necessary to prepare them for what eventually could come.

The kids came up to me one afternoon, and one of them said, "Hey, Mom, we've been talking and now we think we know why you got cancer. It was an exercise," all three heads bobbing in agreement. "That was just the practice. God was really training us for this—this is the real trial."

I thought their assessment was pretty astute, and I believe that at that moment I laid out the challenge before our family.

"I think you're probably right … Listen, I don't know what else is going to happen to us in the future, but let's make a commitment to God and to each other right now to glorify and praise God no matter what happens. Let's be like Job and Joseph in their trials. Whatever comes, we're not going to give God a black eye or make Him look bad. We're not going to blame Him. We're going to trust Him, OK? God is good—period. This isn't His fault. This is a test, that's all, and I don't know about you, but I'm still competitive enough to want to win!"

All three of my little warriors nodded in agreement, and that became the standard from then on, and really, the true test. At first glance, the physical hardships and emotional strain appeared to be the trial, but in reality, the test was: Could we get through this without denying Christ? Would our faith, which is more important to God than our physical bodies, stand firm? Time would tell.

Even with the initial crisis past, Tim was still in danger. Being on the ventilator made him susceptible to pneumonia. Frequently, he spiked fevers either from picking up an infection or from the damage to his brain. His "thermostat" was off kilter. The Japanese do not have blood-screening methods as sophisticated as the United States, so Tim even picked up hepatitis from his many blood transfusions. Every tube that was stuck into his body was a potential portal of entry for infection.

The hospital started preparing to transfer Tim stateside. A tracheostomy was done so that the vent could more easily be inserted into his airway.

Being immobile was causing a host of problems. Tim was developing blood clots in his legs and there was talk about inserting a Greenfield catheter to stop the clots from reaching the lungs and heart, but in the end, it couldn't be done because Tim was allergic to the dye used in the procedure. They ended up using compression stockings on his legs and medication to thin his blood.

Tim was being fed through a nasogastric tube in his nose, and there was discussion about putting in a more permanent PEG tube in his abdomen. I kept thinking of what Tim had said to me just recently about tubes and all and thought how strange that we had just discussed that type of thing. But, no one asked me what Tim wanted and to be honest, at the time, I was thinking of it as a temporary thing. Tim was going to wake up and get better and then we'd take it out.

But, the PEG tube never materialized in Japan. Evidently, if Tim had been Japanese and had been given this prognosis, they would have just let him die, so I was glad that we were getting out of there. The hospital was wonderful to us, but their way of thinking was so foreign to me. I needed to get Tim home.

I felt so useless sitting there day after day. Once in a while, the nurses would send me down to the in-hospital store for diapers, wipes, or a razor for Tim. Eventually, they let me help bathe his hands and feet. I remember the tiny Japanese nurses giggling over Tim's size 13 feet. Tim is 6 foot 2 inches, and he barely fit in their hospital beds.

I began taking photos of all the nurses who cared for Tim, as well as his doctors. I thought that we'd be stateside when Tim awoke and that he would never know the people who had saved his life. For some reason, they all wanted to stand by Tim's side when I photographed them, so I actually have some photos of Tim in intensive care. By this time, he was looking a bit more like himself. To this day, though, none of us have looked at any of those photographs.

I finally went home. We were going to move, and I was the one who had to make all the arrangements. I asked Robb if he thought that it would be OK if I left, and he assured me that Tim would be fine and that if anything happened, I would know about it immediately. By this time, both my mom and Tim's mom had arrived and had been staying on base, so we all went home together.

It was so depressing to walk into our house, and even more depressing walking into our bedroom. That night, I slept on my side of the bed, alone, hugging Tim's pillow, smelling his cologne, and crying. I believe that I cried myself to sleep almost every night for over six months. I still do from time to time.

The next day, I was given back some of Tim's personal items: his watch, his bike shoes, and his wedding band. His wedding band had been cut off. I put in on and squeezed it until it sort of fit my finger. I wore it that way for months and never had it repaired. For some reason, the break in his ring was symbolic to me of the break in our relationship and family.

The phone rang constantly. Stateside family and friends kept calling to offer help and information about hospitals and doctors. Steve E., our pastor from Desert Springs, called and said, once again, the church was poised to help our family should we decide to return to Phoenix. Barrows Neurological Institute, at St. Josephs' Hospital, was one of the best in the world.

I remarked how much I missed everything about Tim, but especially his wisdom and discernment at the moment. I was used to relying on Tim's judgment and hadn't made any major decisions alone since we got married, and I really didn't trust myself. Steve encouraged me to not rush into any decision. He said, "When the time finally comes to make those big decisions, Carole, God will give you the wisdom you need."

Steve was speaking from experience having lost his first wife, Pam, during the birth of their son. He'd started on the path that I was now walking and had had to make some of the same types of decisions that I was facing. I highly respect Steve and took his advice, which has turned out to be true time and time again.

After meeting with the head of civilian personnel and learning of our options, I was finally able to come to a decision about where to move our family.

Right up until the moment that I met with the director of civilian personnel, I still had no idea where our family should move. The military had said they would fly us anywhere we wanted. The director said as far as Tim's position went, we had two options. Tim could be retired immediately from his job with a disability, or, we could exercise our return rights to Luke AFB, keeping Tim on the books until his leave ran out. Then, if Tim didn't recover, he could be retired at that time. Thank you, God, for spelling it out for me. I immediately said, "We're going to Luke. Tim has months and months of leave, and I want to give him as much chance as possible to get better. I'd hate for him to wake up and find that I'd moved our family and lost him his job."

The next few days were pretty stressful, but everyone on the base was so kind and helpful. Tim was actually the one who was sponsored by our government to be in Japan—we were merely his dependents, so Tim's the one who had the authority to sign papers, move us, etc. We were in trouble from the start. The first thing I was asked was, "Do you have a power of attorney for each other?" We didn't. That basically meant I had no right to do any of the things that Tim was supposed to do for us.

The second problem I had was ignorance. Tim and I have always had pretty clear cut, comfortable roles in our home, and we trusted each other to handle our differing areas. My domain was our home and the kids. Tim brought home the bacon, handled the maintenance of the cars, the house, the yard. He handled our bills and finances. We were a "Leave it to Beaver" family.

In Japan, Tim took care of our banking and bills, which involved two banks—one on base and one off base. Our bills were all paid in person, and once or twice a month, Tim would drive around Misawa to pay the rent, insurance, and utilities. I had no idea which of the local banks Tim used or where he paid any of our bills. Tim's organizational style was, how do I put it, less than neat, and as I looked over his desk and files, I couldn't tell which bills were paid and which were still outstanding. Our checkbook wasn't up to date. Then, come to find out, I wasn't even listed on either of our vehicle titles. Legally, I couldn't sell our cars!

I can remember remarking once to Tim that we ought to sit down and go over all those sorts of things together. He agreed, but we never got around to it. Tim would always tease, "I got it all under control. Don't worry your pretty little head over it. Just go paint your nails or something. You're my trophy wife, my arm candy, remember?"

He was truly teasing and not being condescending at all, but his point was clear. It's my job to take care of you and the kids.

I met with one of the lawyers from the JAG and he gave me what came to be known as my "Power Letter." This was a letter signed by the Commander of the 35th Fighter Wing, and it said:

Mr. Timothy Jones, HAWC, was recently rendered legally incompetent due to an accident. On or about 20 Aug 03, Mr. Jones will be medically airlifted to Luke Air Force Base. Mr. Jones will be accompanied by his wife, Mrs. Carole Jones.

Due to Mr. Jones' sudden incompetence, Mrs. Jones has no power of attorney or other documentation to allow her to out-process Misawa Air Base. To the extent permitted by law, this memo serves as authority for Mrs. Jones, or her designated representative, to handle any and all affairs with agencies at Misawa Air Base on behalf of her husband.

The Jones family is going through a trying period. Misawa Air Base will assist the family to the fullest extent possible.

Talk about a done deal. I was given a list of places to go and people to see, and I walked into department after department introducing myself with this letter and people jumped. I'm not sure, but I might have been able to part the Red Sea with that letter, it was so effective!

A quick learner, I immediately gave my mom power of attorney in case anything was to happen to me. I know, I know … what are the chances, right? My mom was such a blessing. She went everywhere with me and served as my secretary, taking notes at the meetings, being an extra pair of ears, asking questions. If I thought she was putting her oar in the water too much, I'd tease her and say, "Hey, I'm a grown up. You're not the boss of me!"

At this she'd start fumbling through a file of papers producing her power of attorney, wave it in the air, and say triumphantly, "Oh, yes I am!"

From then on, things went fairly smoothly. I located our Japanese bank, and accompanied by a Japanese friend, inquired how to close our account. The bank was concerned about the legality of what I was trying to do, but my power letter seemed to do the trick there, as well. Robb and Merry offered to take care of selling our cars, and the Japanese government said they would allow me to sell them for Tim. We even got an immediate appointment to pack out—that's rare, and that was God. Most everything was taken care of in the two weeks before I left with Tim.

At one point, someone told me that I should start the process of filing an insurance claim, so we met with a Japanese national who worked at the JAG office and who was in the claims department. He explained how insurance companies worked in this situation, and it was at this point that we first heard that Tim was supposedly responsible for the accident because he failed to yield at a stop sign. Kay and the girls were with us at this meeting, and they went ballistic.

"My dad did not do that! He's like ... Mr. Safety! He's always getting on us to slow down and be more safe. He always makes us wear helmets, and he's a Driver Ed. teacher! He wouldn't have done that" The kids were angry and defensive.

I agreed that it would be out of character for Tim to fail to yield, and as the conversation progressed, we found out that the woman who struck Tim had admitted to speeding and that there were no witnesses other than the driver and her husband. Tim couldn't tell us his side of the story, so I guess we'll never know what really happened.

I tracked down the police report. My mom and I sat down to look at it one evening after the kids were put to bed. The report said the witnesses claimed that Tim blew through a stop sign and pulled out right in front of them. The driver was going too fast (over 50 mph) and slammed on her brakes, skidding 80 feet before hitting Tim.

As Tim was struck, the front of her car was totaled, and he flew off his bike and smashed into the windshield. After that, he was thrown through the air over 30 feet onto the road. I'd been on this particular bike route with Tim once. It was out near the ocean, and I imagine that morning it was a bit foggy and the roads were probably slick. I know the corner where the accident occurred, and it was a dangerous one. So often, I have vividly pictured Tim riding his bike moments before impact, and I've wondered if he saw it coming. Did he feel or think anything, or was he knocked immediately unconscious? If he had time to think of something, did he think of me or his kids? The poor guy never had a chance.

13

"Going Home"

o o o o o o o o o o o o o o o o o o o o o o o o o o o o o o o o

"I lift up my eyes to the hills—
where does my help come from?
My help comes from the Lord,
the maker of heaven and earth."
Psalm 121:1–2

Tim's fever was still up and down, so we weren't able to medivac him yet. I discovered something while looking at Tim's chest X-ray—his right clavicle was broken, too! I don't think anyone had caught that yet. Not bad for a rookie. On the encouraging side—one test they performed to check his brain stem showed a tiny improvement. I was elated. Now don't get me wrong, the activity was still very minimal, and definitely not normal, but for me it was a small victory.

It was difficult to discern whether Tim's movements were a direct response to what we did and said, or whether they were, as the doctors put it, just reflexive. However, he definitely had a pain response. Occasionally, the nurses let me help wash his hands. One of his hands had a broken bone, and even though we were being very careful, Tim kept jerking his arm. He didn't react that way with the other hand. Often, we would be asked to step out of ICU for a while, so that the medical staff could do some work on Tim. Upon returning we noticed Tim was breathing very quickly, and his BP and HR were extremely high. It was as if he was upset. I would stroke his head and talk to him, and within seconds he seemed to calm down. And what's more, when I kissed him his heart rate went back up! After twenty years, I still had it! Things like that kept our spirits up.

One day, the couple driving the van that collided with Tim was at Tim's bedside when we arrived. They brought us some beautiful flowers and a gift. It was difficult to understand each other's words because of the language barrier, but the tears shed that morning clearly communicated the pain we were all feeling.

These days, I was literally running from dawn to dusk. I would get up and start packing or begin running one of the many errands involved in our move. Then, I'd make the forty-five-minute drive to Hachinohe to be with Tim. After several hours, I'd make the trip back home, get more work done, and go to bed. My insomnia was cured by the exhaustion that I felt.

A lot of cancer survivors often suffer from extreme fatigue for up to a year after battling cancer, but that had never been the case with me. I bounced right back. Now, I realized why God had given me such a tremendous recovery. These past few weeks had been extremely taxing, and had I been sickly after cancer treatment, I might have ended up in the hospital bed next to Tim.

Tim was eventually moved out of ICU and put in a step-down unit. He was breathing spontaneously, so the vent was removed. He was still fighting something, but the doctors made it sound like he could be transported soon.

August 23, 2003

Dear Family and Friends,

Mom and Dad left this morning for Phoenix. They will have stops at Tripler AFB in Hawaii and Travis AFB in California before landing at Luke. Please pray that they will have a safe trip, especially Daddy. **

Rachel, Daniel, and I will leave with our grandmother on Thursday. Thank you all for your continued prayers and support,
Love,
Becky

***The flight would be historic in that Tim would be the first person to be medivaced over the Pacific Ocean on a ventilator.*

Tim was finally well enough to travel. Plans were made to leave first thing the next morning. Kay had already left for Florida and my mom was staying on with the kids to wrap up our move and bring them back to the states. I'd barely seen the kids the last couple of weeks and I hated to leave them, but they were getting in some last minute time with their good friends and I knew they would be all right. Becky, Rachel, and Melody sang in a group together, and they had an opportunity to record a CD during this time. It was a great opportunity for them as well as a distraction.

Merry took me to the base hospital early the next morning where we waited for Tim and his American team of doctors to arrive. As I signed some papers I remember that Col. Pete H., who had been one of the doctors who frequently sat in on the meetings with the Japanese neurosurgeons, assured me that he'd found a regulation somewhere allowing the military to medivac Tim without any cost to us. I thanked him profusely then, and I thank him now, because I have since learned that the flight cost more than $20,000.

Tim's ambulance arrived and as we headed for the plane we saw a number of Tim's co-workers and friends from the base lined up on either side of the path that Tim's stretcher would follow. It was a demonstration of love and respect that touched me deeply.

Dr. Liing C., a surgeon whom I had gotten to know quite well over the past few weeks, and Capt. Sharon W., an anesthesiologist, were to accompany us. Tim had been weaned from the vent, but they put him back on it for the trip. We were on a C135, and it had been modified so that Tim could be transported on a stretcher. It was sort of like having a little hospital in one corner of the plane. There were also some regular airplane seats and a few other passengers.

The flight went well. Some of the crew lent me a spot to stretch out and sleep and later gave me a tour of the plane. I forget what it was called, but there is a place underneath the plane that you can crawl into and look out through some windows while laying on your stomach. It was spectacular—the sun was rising over the ocean in a glorious display of colors, and as I lay there I felt very small and insignificant in the scope of things. The knowledge that the God who made the sun and the great sea was, at that very moment, completely concerned about Tim and me—and that He was with us!—was pretty amazing to me.

August 30, 2003

Dear Family and Friends,

Just a quick update—we're home, praise God. After five days, we finally arrived in Phoenix Thursday evening.

Tim did pretty well, but the trip was hard on his respiratory system and he's been struggling with pneumonia and high fevers. He is in critical condition in the trauma ICU unit at St. Joseph's hospital. They have found a couple of new things that need to be dealt with, but it is late and I will tell you about it next time. Pastor Steve and

Tami E. have graciously taken us in again. We stayed with them when I began cancer treatment last year.

In fact, we arrived at their house exactly one year ago to the day. I commented, "Didn't we just <u>do</u> this?"

14

"A New Reality"

o o o o o o o o o o o o o o o o o o o o o o o o o o o o o o o o o o

Psalm 138:8

"The Lord will fulfill His purpose for me; Your love, O Lord, endures forever—do not abandon the works of Your hands."

By the time we got to Phoenix, Tim's condition had regressed. He'd developed pneumonia during the trip, his fever was quite high again, and he needed more help breathing from the ventilator. He also seemed less responsive. The doctors began evaluating Tim's condition, and one thing they discovered that had apparently been missed in Japan was that Tim had fractures in his cervical vertebrae (broken bones in the neck). God really protected Tim in that none of the fractures moved any bones out of place, so the spinal column was not affected. How thankful I was that Dr. C. insisted on putting Tim back into a cervical collar for the trip!

The doctors did another CT scan and it appeared that fluid was beginning to build up in the brain again. Tim had surgery so that the doctor's could put in a permanent shunt to control the fluid on his brain. Other than inserting a Greenfield catheter to catch blood clots and providing Tim with a more permanent feeding tube, the doctors held off doing any other surgeries on Tim. A month had passed since the accident and Tim's other injuries were healing on their own. If Tim awakened he would need more surgeries to get the full use of his body back, but at the time he wasn't going anywhere and there didn't seem to be any reason to subject him to any more than he'd already been through.

Within the first week at St. Joe's, Tim's doctors felt that it was their responsibility to bring me down to reality. One day, a neurologist somberly informed me that Tim would never regain consciousness. Then, they kept me waiting all day to meet with another neurologist who desperately needed to speak with me about

Tim's condition. It was an agonizing day because I'd been led to believe that at this next meeting I would be forced to make a decision where Tim's life was concerned. As I mentioned before, Tim wasn't brain dead, and up to this point no one had ever come to me and asked if Tim should continue to be treated. I truly thought the moment of truth had come and that they were going to tell me to pull the plug on Tim.

When the neurologist finally showed up, it wasn't even Tim's neurologist, but some mere rookie, and he basically told me exactly the same thing that I'd been hearing from day one.

Vegetative state, may be able to follow some simple commands, but no consciousness ever again.

At first I was kind of mad at them, and then, of course, I was relieved. Still, continually hearing that Tim would never recover was so devastating. The worst part about it was how this terrible news was delivered. The docs walked up to you and basically said, "he's broke and we can't fix him. Sorry," and then they strode right out the door. It was as if someone had pulled the pin on a live grenade and handed it to you! Your life blew up and you were left standing there, wounded and shattered, wondering what in the world you were supposed to do. I stood there crying on my pastor's shoulder for a really long time, just saying over and over, "What do I do now?"

Come to find out, the doctor's were confused by my response to Tim's condition. Because I continued to talk and interact with Tim and speak hopefully about his recovery, they seemed to feel that I wasn't facing reality. They didn't realize that I did fully comprehend everything they told me, and that from a human standpoint, there was little hope. However, I could face reality without losing my faith in God. I couldn't say that I knew for sure what God was going to do. But, I felt that He would not leave Tim in a coma. I knew that nothing was impossible for God. The head of Tim's trauma care had said, "We've done everything that we can possibly do, and now we wait and see what kind of a result we'll get." That's all I was doing.

As the days passed, we began to see more movement from Tim. Facial expressions, such as grimacing when the respiratory nurse came into the room and loudly announced that it was time to give Tim a breathing treatment, or seeming attempts to squeeze our hand or open his eyes when asked. Each was a glorious victory in my view. The doctors never shared my elation, though, and I couldn't understand why.

They also told me that Tim wasn't a good candidate for neurological rehabilitation at Barrow's until he was alert and able to consistently follow commands. It began to look like Tim would be heading to an extended care facility.

Dear Family and Friends,

Yesterday was another encouraging day. I guess the Lord knows when you need encouragement. When I went in to visit Tim, he was resting comfortably on his left side with his eyes closed. As I began to talk to him, his right eye looked like it was opening a little. The only time that I've seen him open his right eye is in response to pain. I continued to talk to him and slowly his right eye opened halfway. I can't say for sure if he saw me or saw anything, but sometimes I would reach towards him to stroke his forehead, and his eye would blink slightly. Needless to say, I was on cloud nine for the rest of the day.

I was able to go to church today for the first time since the accident. It was inspirational. Some of the songs were a little hard to sing without tears, but it was so good to be back with our church family. Pastor Steve just happened to be teaching on Luke 22, the passage where Christ tells Peter that Satan had obtained permission to sift him like wheat. Boy, can we relate! When I was diagnosed with cancer, Tim said to me that he thought that whole ordeal could have been some sort of spiritual attack. I remember saying, "Why would the enemy waste his time on me?"

But honestly, as soon as this happened to Tim, a spiritual "Job-like" attack was the first thing that came to mind. I pray constantly for protection for my family. I would really specifically like prayer for one thing: that our family would be able to walk through this trial without losing faith, or damaging God's character. Sometimes it is easy to feel overwhelmed by the circumstances around us. We are so helped and strengthened by your prayers.

A mighty fortress is our God
A bulwark never failing
Our helper He amidst the flood
Of mortal ills prevailing
For still our ancient foe
Doth seek to work us woe
His craft and power are great
And armed with cruel hate
On earth is not his equal

Did we in our own strength confide,
Our striving would be losing;

Were not the right Man on our side,
The Man of God's own choosing:
Dost ask who that may be?
Christ Jesus, it is He;
Lord Sabaoth His Name,
From age to age the same,
And He must win the battle.

And though this world, with devils filled,
Should threaten to undo us;
We will not fear, for God hath willed
His truth to triumph through us:
The prince of darkness grim,
We tremble not for him;
His rage we can endure,
For lo, his doom is sure,
One little word shall fell him.

That word above all earthly pow'rs,
No thanks to them abideth;
The Spirit and the gifts are ours
Through Him Who with us sideth:
Let goods and kindred go,
This mortal life also;
The body they may kill;
God's truth abideth still,
His Kingdom is forever.
—Martin Luther

Please pray that Tim would awaken soon so that he can go to Barrow's, and for me as I deal with all the time-consuming issues that have resulted from this situation.

Peace,
Carole and the Kids

15

"Time Consuming Issues"

o o o o o o o o o o o o o o o o o o o o o o o o o o o o o o o o o o

Psalm 57: 1–2

"Have mercy on me, O, God. Have mercy on me, for in You my soul takes refuge. I will take refuge in the shadow of Your wings until the disaster has passed. I cry out to God most high, to God who fulfills his purpose for me."

Time consuming issues ... where do I start? The first major thing that needed to be done was to go to court to be made Tim's guardian. I was warned in Misawa that once we reached the states that this would be necessary, and one of the majors in the JAG office had started the paperwork for me. This process was extremely time-consuming, expensive, and completely unnecessary as far as I was concerned. I didn't need a piece of paper to tell me to take care of my husband! I already had one—our marriage license with a faithful track record of over twenty years—but that meant nothing to the "powers that be."

Because Tim was still employed at Luke AFB, he needed to be in-processed, and I needed authority to sign papers for him, set up direct deposits, and the like. The entire guardianship process was insulting and degrading. I was made to feel like a gold digger. Our money was frozen and the commissioner assigned to our case actually made some very cutting remarks inferring that I was after "Tim's money."

What money? We had no stocks, bonds, property—only a savings account from the previous sale of our house in Glendale. Tim's money? The words "yours" and "mine" hadn't been a part of our family's vocabulary for 20 years. I left that courthouse frustrated and crying many, many times. It got to the point that when I drove up to that place, I would tense up all over till I was nearly shaking.

A court-appointed lawyer was assigned to Tim. We eventually met at the courthouse prior to a hearing. Paul was a really good guy, and he had already been to see Tim. He assured me that he was on "our" side and had no fears as regards to my character. An investigator was put on our case, and also made a trip to visit Tim in the hospital. I filled out form after form and ran back and forth to the courthouse. Finally, the investigator called to interrogate ... I mean, interview me. She was a pleasant gal and even more appalled than I was at how our case was being handled.

Evidently, Maricopa County where we resided was one of the worst places in the country for elderly abuse. It was quite common for dishonest people to take advantage of someone and to try to get control over their money, so, granted, laws were needed to protect people who couldn't protect themselves.

"But," fumed the investigator, "this isn't the case here! You don't have any assets to speak of; you've been married for 20 years. You're a family for *#@@#$ sake, and you're going through a hard enough time without being treated like this!" God bless her.

After hearing from the investigator, the commissioner softened her tone towards me. She unfroze our accounts and granted the guardianship. At one point, she tried to bond me (just in case I bailed on Tim and took all of our vast wealth and tried to run!). But Paul, bless his heart, stood up and said, "No, that won't be necessary, your Honor."

I never dreamed in a million years that I would be considering a nursing home for my 44-year-old husband, but that was the other issue that I was wrestling with. Tim was ready to be moved, and they were waiting on me to tell them where.

September 11, 2003

Dear Family and Friends,

Long story short: Tim was moved today—just down the hall in St. Joe's! A couple of days ago, we found out about a facility right inside the hospital that could take Tim. It's a hospital within the hospital, and they (and our insurance) are agreeable to taking Tim and even to begin trying some coma stimulation methods to wake him up.

This is really an answer to prayer. I had been dreading the possibility of Tim having to go to a skilled nursing facility, because I was afraid that everyone (doctors) would forget about him there, and that he wouldn't get the help or the rehab that he needed. This gives Tim more time to become more alert. Our prayer is that the tech-

niques that they try will work and that Tim will wake up, get into Barrow's Neuro Rehab, and come home.

He's been moved to the third floor and an interesting note is that his new roommate's (also named Tim) wife had been in a coma years ago for three months and came out of it.

It has been seven weeks today since Tim went into a coma.

September 15, 2003

Deuteronomy 32: 3–4

"I will proclaim the name of the Lord. Oh, praise the greatness of our God! He is the Rock, His works are perfect, and all His ways are just.
A faithful God who does no wrong, upright and just is He."

Dear Family and Friends,

It seems like Tim has good days and bad days. Today was a good one. The therapists are trying to establish a baseline for Tim. They performed some tests on him three days in a row, and I was able to watch two days of the testing. I think it's actually easier for me to gauge his response because I see him every day, and I can tell when something's different.

Today, Tim opened his left eye just a crack. We haven't seen that eye open since the accident occurred. Also, when he yawns or sighs, we can hear a vocal noise. The first time it happened was such a surprise as we haven't heard a noise from him in almost two months. He seemed just a tiny bit startled when they rang a bell close to his head. The therapist said he scored better today than the last two times, so that was encouraging. Other than that, he's steady as a rock, his vitals are good, and he hasn't had a fever since he was transferred to his new room. He just seems more comfortable now that he's not getting poked and prodded as much. Mom and Dad and the kids and I have been taking turns sitting with Tim, and now our church family is going to also.

We're trying to be patient, knowing that progress is really slow with an injury like this. I've been told that the brain is the slowest organ in the whole body to heal. We really miss Tim, though, and the waiting and wondering is hard. We want you to know that your prayers are getting us through. I will take absolutely no credit for having the strength to keep going. All the praise should go to the Lord.

Our only consolation is His character, His Word, His promises, and His Spirit. I really, really don't know how this will turn out, although I constantly pray for a particular outcome. We are trusting completely in God's character—who He is, not what He does for us. He's God and He says that His grace is sufficient for us. We are trust-

ing Him to act according to His character and Word, so we know that whatever happens will be loving, wise, powerful, perfect, and best.

> *"I am God, and there is no other;*
> *I am God, and there is none like me.*
> *I make known the end from the beginning,*
> *from ancient times, what is still to come.*
> *I say: My purpose will stand,*
> *and I will do all that I please."*
> *Isaiah 47: 9–10*

Peace,
Carole and the kids

My dad loves a project, so I gave him one. His job was to find me a decent vehicle while I hunted for an apartment. Each morning, I would get up early and head for the hospital. Usually, one or more of the kids would come with me and we often met up with my parents or someone from church. We'd spend a couple of hours with Tim and then head out to look at apartments.

I was originally looking for a place near the hospital to avoid the two 30-mile round trips I was making every day to St. Joe's. Eventually, though, I realized that it might be better for the kids to be nearer to my folks and our church family out in the West Valley. Also, you got more cluck for your buck out in the West Valley, as far as the quality of houses goes. Mom and Dad finally stumbled across a place in Avondale, and I rented it. While no one said anything, I think everyone breathed a collective sigh of relief knowing that my family would be near by in case we needed help.

September 23, 2003

Dear Family and Friends,

"I strongly suspect that if we saw all the difference even the tiniest of our prayers make, and all the people those little prayers were destined to affect, and all the consequences of those prayers down through the centuries, we would be so paralyzed with awe at the power of prayer that we would be unable to get up off our knees for the rest of our lives."
—Peter Kreeft (quote from *Reader's Digest*)

Our hearts have been so touched by the faithfulness of your prayers. Day after day, through your cards and emails, we are assured of your support and continued prayers. Thank you.

Thank you, too, for your visits with Tim at the hospital. I've been blessed by the comments you have jotted down in the visitor's log. I believe that he is aware of your presence.

Tim got a new roommate. This man had been in a serious motorcycle accident and had actually flat lined twice at the accident scene. He was in a coma for almost three weeks. This week while some of the folks from Desert Springs CC were at the hospital visiting with Tim, they got an opportunity to share the gospel with Tim's roommate, Dean. Dean prayed with them, along with his wife and children, to receive Christ as Savior and Lord. So exciting!

It is so obvious to us that God is working in and through this situation and that lives are being touched. That knowledge strengthens our faith in a God who remains in control.

A few days ago, I received a very encouraging e-mail from our college days pastor and his wife. Two of the scriptures he mentioned were from the book of Luke. The next day, I happened to pick up one of my devotionals and the text that day contained the same verses. Our pastor had shared the verses to encourage me about persistence in prayer—even to the point of badgering God. I wrote back and said, "I can do that!" I appreciate all of you for "badgering" the Lord with us. I know God hears us and that He is moved by entreaty.

In His hands,

Carole and the Kids

Luke 11: 5–9

Luke 18: 1–8

"However, when the Son of Man comes, will He find faith on the earth?" Will He find the faith which banks on Him in spite of the confusion? Stand off in faith believing that what Jesus said is true, though in the meantime you do not understand what God is doing. He has bigger issues at stake than the particular things you ask.

The Strangeness of His Faithfulness, by Oswald Chambers

Tim began receiving drugs that were intended to stimulate him to wake up. I'd been reading up on the whole idea of coma stimulation and evidently it wasn't a proven practice, but the reasoning behind it made sense to me. Besides, we felt that we had nothing to lose by giving it a try.

Therapists were working Tim hard, trying to get him to respond. Because his responses were delayed sometimes 15 seconds or more, it wasn't clear if he was doing what we asked or randomly moving. Being an overly optimistic person, I saw every response as purposeful. All of us did and Tim's therapists were encouraging and said Tim was making very slight progress.

Many people were confused at how Tim could still be considered comatose and yet be responsive to commands and even open his eyes. When you walked into his room, he looked awake. I didn't completely understand it either, but from what I did understand, there were different levels of a coma. When Tim first entered the hospital, he was considered to be in an extreme coma. Now, he was considered to be in a moderate coma. Progress was excruciatingly slow—but hey, progress *was* progress.

James 5: 16b–18
"The prayer of a righteous man is powerful and effective. Elijah was a man just like us. He prayed earnestly that it would not rain, and it did not rain on the land for three and a half years.
Again he prayed, and the heavens gave rain,
and the earth produced its crops."

October 11, 2003

Dear Family and Friends,
I know that you all have been wondering what is happening with us. The kids and I have been moving in and unpacking these past few days. It is good to be out of suitcases and boxes.

Tim is holding steady. Vitals are very good and his lungs have been really clear. He opens both eyes now when you start talking to him (most of the time) and he moves his left arm, hand, and leg. He still responds inconsistently, but this past week he seemed to try to pucker up when I asked him to. We have a lot of questions for his various doctors, but they are hard to track down, and I am hoping to set up a meeting with our case manager to get our questions answered by this week. I can't believe that Tim will have been in a coma for three months this Thursday.

We're so thankful to be settling into our house.

We have leased a smallish four-bedroom house in the West Valley. We all agree it's just right for us, except that it is missing one thing—Tim. We hope and pray he'll be able to come home soon.

Our subdivision has many little man-made lakes and we have one of the lakes right behind our back fence. Daniel has been trying so hard to catch a fish since we moved in—but no luck so far.

The Lord was good to us again as both of our household shipments were delivered the day after we moved into the house. My folks were a tremendous help in unpacking and setting up. We were out of boxes in two days. Rebecca hooked up both computers, the stereo, TV, VCR and DVD player, and she did it right! Do you suppose I could hire her out?

This whole situation (moving, setting up a household, running all of our family affairs) has been such a learning experience for me. Most of the time I feel like I am supposed to be a jack of all trades when I'm really a master of none. So, I'd appreciate your prayers as I muddle along.

We are amazed—amazed—at God's continual care, provision, and encouragement towards our family. I admit I have been so very tired, wondering how in the world I am going to last the duration of this, but God continually reminds me through His people, and His Word, and answered prayer that He's listening, He cares, and He will provide grace to meet each day's demands.

Lamentations 3:22 and 23 says,
"Because of the Lord's great love we are not consumed, for His compassions never fail.
They are new every morning; great is Your faithfulness."

In Christ,
Carole

16

"Not My Own"

It was a little easier on the kids to move into a brand new place. It had been the four of us for quite a while now, but it still seemed so odd. Even though Tim's clothes, photographs, and possessions were all around us, he had never been in this house. We had no memories of Tim in this place.

As I mentioned before, I spent a lot of time at the hospital each day accompanied by our kids. I tried to take them singly so that I could have a chance to talk with them alone. The months were passing and they were hurting, wondering if Daddy would ever get to come home. Sometimes, we'd grab lunch and I would encourage them to talk about how they were feeling. The girls were able to express themselves very well. Dan was full of questions. For some reason, he would ask me the same questions periodically. The question he always asked me first dealt with time travel.

"Mommy," he'd say, "If you could go back in time, what day would you go back to?" I always answered, "I'd go back to the day before your dad's accident." He'd smile and say, "Me, too!" Then I'd say, in an effort to keep that smile on his face, "That way we could tie him up and puncture both of his bike tires!" He'd really grin at that. I think it made him feel better to know that if somehow we could have prevented Tim's accident, we would have.

The other thing he always asked me was, "Mommy, if Daddy goes to heaven will you marry somebody else and put his pictures away?"

Every time he asked me that, it nearly broke my heart. I think he needed assurance of some sort, so I would always answer, "Danny, no one could ever, ever replace your daddy. And, honey, I want you to know that we will always keep your dad's pictures out no matter what happens. In fact, you can have any pictures of your dad for your bedroom that you want, OK?"

He'd smile at that and dig back into his cheeseburger and fries.

For three months, our family had walked around as if we had all been put into a coma. No one felt like doing anything fun because we felt guilty about being OK when Tim was not.

Finally I said one evening, "Gee, we're not dead, so let's stop acting like it! Get your coats! I called Grandma and Grandpa and they are meeting us at the movies."

We tried to enjoy ourselves that evening, but it didn't seem right and we all felt it. I remember crying in front of the kids most of the way home.

Time would eventually help in that, and eventually we became pretty used to the four of us being a family.

October 18, 2003

Dear Family and Friends,
The bad news is that there hasn't been anything new to report on Tim.
His progress has plateaued lately.
The good news is that God is still in control, His promise in Romans 8:28 is still in effect, and His grace is still sufficient for whatever we are facing. Best of all, we still have eternal life.
Please stop thinking I'm some sort of super saint who never feels discouraged. Let me tell you that I write these things to remind myself of the truth. Daily, even minute by minute, I make the choice to believe what God says in His word about Himself, or I succumb to worry, fear, and my unpredictable feelings.

Carole

The acute neural rehab doctor assigned to Tim said he was considered a level 2 on the Rancho Los Amigos Coma Scale. Level 1 was no response at all. Level 2 was a generalized response to external stimuli. Tim made some responses, but they were always the same and not necessarily directly related to what he was asked to do. Making it to Level 3 would be a big improvement. At that level people made specific responses, even though they were delayed and inconsistent. There were eight levels that people progressed through when coming out of a coma. Tim's doctor wanted him to make it to a level three, if possible—and soon, too. The longer someone stayed at a level two, the more likely they'd remain there.

I got discouraged sometimes—but I realized that my real problem was my tendency to forget that my life was not my own. I forgot that my life belonged to God. He bought and paid for me with His precious Son's blood.

So often, we Christians think we're put here on earth just to settle for the American Dream. We make plans for a nice, comfy life—nice house, spouse, kids, car, pocketbook, health. We forget that we're here to glorify God, and that it's His choice, and not ours, how best that can be accomplished.

To be quite honest, I would have loved my comfortable life back. I wasn't having much fun lately. But, I knew that God had plans for my life, too, and His plans were better than my plans.

While He didn't cause this to happen to my family, He permitted it, and we had His unbreakable word that He would use it to accomplish His good, loving, and perfect purpose in our lives.

1 Sam. 27:1
"And David said in his heart, I shall now perish one day by the hand of Saul."
The thought of David's heart at this time was a false thought, because he certainly had no ground for thinking that God's anointing him by Samuel was intended to be left as an empty unmeaning act. On no one occasion had the Lord deserted His servant; he had been placed in perilous positions very often, but not one instance had occurred in which divine interposition had not delivered him. The trials to which he had been exposed had been varied;
they had not assumed one form only, but many—yet in every case He who sent the trial had also graciously ordained a way of escape.
David could not put his finger upon any entry in his diary, and say of it, "Here is evidence that the Lord will forsake me," for the entire tenor of his past life proved the very reverse. He should have argued from what God had done for him, that God would be his defender still. But is it not just in the same way that we doubt God's help? Is it not mistrust without a cause?
Have we ever had the shadow of a reason to doubt our Father's goodness? Have not His loving kindnesses been marvelous? Has He once failed to justify our trust? Ah, no! Our God has not left us at any time.
We have had dark nights, but the star of love shone forth amid the blackness; we have been in stern conflicts, but over our head He has held aloft the shield of our defense. We have gone through many trials, but never to our detriment, always to our advantage; and the conclusion from our past experience is, that He who has been with us in six troubles, will not forsake us in the seventh. What we have known of our faithful God proves that He will keep us to the end. Let us not, then, reason contrary to evi-

dence. How can we ever be so ungenerous as to doubt our God? Lord, throw down the Jezebel of our unbelief, and let the dogs devour it.
                    —Charles Spurgeon

Dan celebrated his 11th birthday on October 21. I took the kids to the State Fair. We had never been to it before. We watched the Wild West Show and rode some of the carnival rides. Dan declared the evening to be "his best birthday ever" (except, he said, that daddy wasn't there). Oh, Dan also finally hooked a big fish that week—unfortunately, it got away. Really. I was a witness. The hook slid right off. Still, he was thrilled to finally get one on his line.

Early in November, we were able to spend time with some dear friends we had met in Misawa, Japan. Bobbi and Dennis C. and their family drove down from New Mexico where they had relocated after leaving Japan. We hadn't seen them since my family went stateside for my cancer treatment. Melody D., our dear friend who still lived in Misawa, visited at the same time. It was such a treat for the kids to be back together.

Melody, Becky and Rachel, and Julianna C. had formed a quartet called Souled Out while we were all living in Japan. That Sunday, at our church, Souled Out sang together for the first time in over a year. It was very special. Becky gave a short testimony before they sang their second song called "Blue Skies." She said the words to the song were so true and that even though her family had been through some very grave times lately, nothing changed the fact that God was good. She said He is good today, He was good yesterday, and He will always be good.

It really blessed my heart to hear those words as my "mother's prayer" for our kids the past few years had been for my children's faith to be genuine and their very own—not just an inherited faith from their parents. I guess there is really no way to know for sure if something is authentic, like faith, unless it is tested.

I definitely didn't have all the answers and I didn't know for sure why this had happened. I am sure there were a number of reasons, and some of them probably didn't even specifically pertain to my family. I received a booklet from some friends called *Some Things I Learned About God From the Life of Joseph*. It was really encouraging and I read it to Tim and the kids. Joseph was probably Tim's favorite person (next to the Lord) in all of scripture. Anyway, one thing mentioned really caught my attention. The author said often times we go through trials for the benefit of other people. I hadn't really thought of that, but agreed with it. Whatever the reason(s), Tim would say that if it was OK with the Lord, it was OK with him. I just wished I was always OK with it!

17

"Change"

o o o o o o o o o o o o o o o o o o o o o o o o o o o o o o o o o

I am the Lord, I change not. Malachi 3:6

I liked Tim's neural rehab doctor—she had a very positive outlook, and faith that Tim could improve, although she couldn't say how much. Talk about refreshing.

After one of Tim's sessions I was talking with the therapist. She commented that his responses were still so inconsistent that it was difficult to know for sure what was purposeful and what wasn't. I told her that was my biggest frustration, too. Just the other day, I asked Tim to do some things that were different from his usual responses. He usually squeezed his hand, moved his thumb, lifted his head off the pillow, opened his eyes, moved his foot, and it seemed to be in response to our asking.

But, if you watched him, he did those things at other times even when no one asked him. The neurosurgeons insisted that Tim's usual movements were simply reflexive. So, I'd been working with him to try to see if I could get him to do something "new." Opening his eyes could be construed as a reflexive movement, but shutting his eyes couldn't. So I began to ask Tim to shut his eyes. At the time, his eyes were wide open, and he was blinking only occasionally. As I watched him, he began to blink more rapidly, and then 45 seconds later, he scrunched his eyes closed for a second. I had been very excited, and as I told the therapist this I said, "And since then, I haven't been able to get him to do that again. Now I wonder if it really was a response after all."

She said, "Exactly." The truth was, we really didn't know.

◆   ◆   ◆

In my mind and heart I was hoping that by three months Tim would be out of the coma. The longer he remained in a coma, the less likely he was to awaken. By the four-month mark, Tim's abilities had reached a plateau and a family meeting was held with all of Tim's doctors and therapists at Select. I initially thought this meeting was to tell us that they'd tried and it just wasn't working. Dr. K. (acute neural rehab) was tenacious and confident and didn't strike me as someone who gave up too quickly—did I mention that I liked her?

At the meeting, Dr. K. explained that she was giving Tim three different drugs (Provigil, Amantadine, and Straltera) that were theoretically supposed to increase Tim's level of consciousness. She described Tim as being "minimally conscious."

Then, the other therapists shared their perceptions, and we talked about plans for Tim's future. I was told that I had two choices to consider. Select Specialty Hospital was a hospital, and Tim couldn't stay there much longer because he wasn't "sick." I could choose to take Tim down to Barrow's Neurological Institute for acute rehab immediately, and after he finished there, we could take him home.

The other choice was to place Tim in a skilled nursing facility to give him more time to progress, if possible, and then at a later date, take him to Barrow's and then home. The gist of their questions boiled down to: "If Tim's condition didn't change from what it was today, what did I plan to do?"

A couple of key things helped me in the decision that I eventually made. Dr. K. explained that if I chose to have Tim at Barrow's right now, the therapy would be more for me than it would be for Tim. They would basically prepare me for taking care of him when he came home. Tim had not progressed enough to participate in his therapy—the therapists basically did therapy *to* Tim.

If we gave Tim more time to heal and make progress, he could enter Barrow's later on when the therapy would benefit him more. Insurance companies only gave you so many days for certain types of therapy, and I didn't want Tim's days used up if they weren't really benefiting him. Also, to bring Tim home I would need to make some changes to the house. I explained that I was leasing a home so I couldn't make the necessary changes. I needed time to get us a permanent home, and Tim needed more time to get better.

I was really thankful to God. Once again, He was so faithful in that when the time came to make a big decision, the wisdom that I needed was provided. This was a day that I had been dreading and dreading. As soon as they started talking about placing Tim in a skilled nursing facility, I could feel the tears stinging my eyes. But, this move was not necessarily permanent.

The very next day, Dad and Becky and I visited a place (Palm Valley Rehabilitation and Care) that was only five minutes from where the kids and I lived, and it was very, very nice. I had prayed and prayed all that night and morning that we would find someplace nice, available, close to our home, and not smelly. (I had visited two other nursing homes, and one of them just stunk.)

November 11, 2003

I can't believe how our lives have changed in the past 16 weeks. We live in a completely different country, a different house, drive a different car, and even have a different dog. Our family roles have changed with Mom pinch-hitting for Daddy as the bill payer, car washer, catcher for Danny's pitching, and spiritual leader.

We have new routines. Everything has changed.

It seems that each week, God instills into my heart ONE thing that makes the difference in my attitude and outlook. Last week, it was being reminded of how much Tim loved the life of Joseph in the Bible. I had been struggling with feeling not so badly for myself, but with feeling so badly for Tim and all that he has to endure. But, God reminded me of the many, many times that Tim would quote Genesis 50. Joseph's brothers were afraid that after their father died Joseph would bear a grudge against them and try to get even for the awful things they had done to him.

Joseph's response was, "You meant evil against me, but God meant it for good in order to bring about this present result."

Tim would constantly tell us, "God is in control." That was a comforting thought for me last week, because I knew that Tim, if he could speak, would be reminding me of that.

This week, as I think about all the changes that we have gone through recently, I am reminded that in the midst of all this change, two things can definitely be counted on.

First, we can count on the fact that things will change. Life is never really the same from one day to the next. The weather changes (it is raining today in Phoenix), our age changes, our health changes, even our hair changes. Why, six months ago I was completely bald and now I have hair! Every day this week as I have driven to the hospital and prayed about my time with Tim, I have reminded myself that this day could be different. Something could change today.

It is encouraging to know that all trials end. Some trials last a little longer than others, but they all eventually end—either in this life or the life to come. Some day, life will be different for us.

The other thing we can count on in the midst of change is the fact that God doesn't change. I love that fact that each and every word of the Bible is inspired by God. There isn't a careless word to be found anywhere. So, when the Bible says, "God's mercies are new every morning" or "I will never leave you or forsake you" or "My grace IS sufficient (complete) for you," that He really means just that!

His words are just as true today as when they were written thousands of years ago. And I am so grateful to Him to still be standing sixteen weeks after the worst day of my life. You prop us up with your prayers, and God consoles us deep down where no one else can see or reach with His changeless, unwavering loving kindness and faithfulness.

Now to Him who is able to keep you from stumbling,
And to make you stand in the presence of His glory
blameless with great joy,
To the only God our Savior,
through Jesus Christ our Lord,
Be glory, majesty, dominion, and authority,
before all time, now and forevermore.
Amen!
Jude 24, 25

Love,
Carole and the Kids

Tim's roommates came and went. I got to see firsthand two men come out of comas.

One of the men had been in a coma for two weeks, and I think the other had been in a coma even longer than that. I was really glad for them and for their families, but often it was hard not to feel pangs of jealousy. I kept wondering, "Why not Tim?"

One of the guys that Tim roomed with was kind of a jerk, too. He had a wife that visited him in the hospital, and a girlfriend! I had some words with the Lord over that one. Life didn't seem fair when someone like Tim didn't recover and less than honorable people did. But the Lord was quick to remind me that if I wanted to be treated fairly, if I really wanted to receive what was due me, I'd be on my merry way to hell in a heartbeat.

"All have sinned" (Romans 3:23) and none of us deserve God's goodness. I don't remember the Bible saying anywhere that life would be fair. Just the opposite, in fact.

I was struck by the difference in Tim's abilities and his recovering roommates. As his roomies came out of their comas, their responses became more consistent and you could see a definite attempt at communication. Often, the nurses would ask the recovering patient a question and they would answer "yes" with a thumbs up. Tim could sometimes give you a thumbs up when you asked him, but he couldn't answer questions or use his thumb to communicate.

November 13, 2003

Today was very special for me because Daniel was finally himself at Daddy's room. Ever since the accident, Dan has been so very quiet whenever we visit his daddy. He practically speaks in whispers and acts almost afraid to come near to Tim's bedside. I think it's totally understandable. Dad doesn't look or act like he used to, and it is probably pretty scary for an 11 year old to behold.

I have been trying to encourage Daniel to talk to his dad, but even that is upsetting, I think, because Tim doesn't respond. Today, I was talking to Tim and re-hanging pictures in his new room, and Dan was putting pictures up on the bulletin board. He turned to his dad and said, "Hey, Daddy, can you give me a thumbs up?" Tim gave him a thumbs up, and Dan got very excited. It sort of broke the ice. Next thing I know, Dan was teasing his dad, and he even hugged Tim when he left.
Love,
Carole

Tim was transferred to Palm Valley Rehabilitation and Care December 1. I really wanted and planned for Tim to come home someday. I constantly wished that Tim and I were some cute little old couple in our seventies, with grown kids and grandkids because then I wouldn't feel torn between taking care of Tim and taking care of our kids.

I knew that if Tim came home now, I would become his primary caregiver 24 hours a day, seven days a week. I knew that Tim would require so much care that I wouldn't be available to help the kids with school, watch their sports, see their church programs, and basically watch them grow up. They were already missing one parent, and I didn't want to deprive them of another.

I knew, too, that Tim's care was so comprehensive and complicated that I would be afraid to be responsible for it. I was pretty in tune with him, but he wasn't aware and couldn't communicate at all, and the potential for disaster in his situation was extremely high. Tim really needed the constant care of a trained nurse.

Our families were dealing with some of the same issues with our elderly grandparents and no one wanted to see me in that situation.

Finally, I thought about how Tim would feel. I knew that he wouldn't want his children's final memories of him to be them helping change their dad's diaper.

The time wasn't right yet for Tim to come home. I prayed that God would enable Tim to communicate consistently. Then, we'd bring him home.

18

"Losing Ground"

Between the kids and me, my folks, and our church family, someone was in Tim's room off and on all day. We liked the folks at PV—they were very attentive to Tim and very compassionate.

Unfortunately, Tim developed a bad urinary tract infection and became quite ill. On top of this, his feeding tube came out a few days after moving to PV and we had to spend all evening at the ER only to be told that they couldn't replace his tube that evening. We returned Tim to PV, and the next morning Dad went back to the ER with Tim at about 10 am. (I had my cancer checkup). I joined Dad later on, and we waited all day for Tim's tube to finally be replaced. We finally got Tim back to PV about 9:30 p.m. All the moving around was very difficult on Tim.

He became totally unresponsive once he became ill. The therapists wanted to work with him, but he was so sick that everything was put on hold until he got better. He was on two different antibiotics and pain meds, as well as his usual medications. They started giving him oxygen because he was very congested and breathing so rapidly—it seemed like breathing was a lot of work for him.

I knew that when someone was in Tim's condition that each infection was harder and harder on his body. He'd been on antibiotics for months, and that tended to produce resistant bugs, which became increasingly difficult to knock out. I sometimes wondered how much more his body could take. He'd lost 45 lbs. since the accident.

Pastor Steve and some dear folks from our church stopped by one evening and anointed Tim with oil and prayed over him. Steve specifically prayed for Tim to be totally healed and home by Christmas, which is what the kids and I had been praying for all along.

Though it had been a hard and discouraging week, we still maintained that God was good, faithful, and worthy of our trust. I had a lot of hard questions for

Him, a lot of strong emotion. He didn't give me any answers, just a calm assurance that He understood and that He would deliver Tim.

"For as the sufferings of Christ abound in us, so our consolation also aboundeth by Christ." 2 Cor. 1:5

"Here is a blessed proportion. The Ruler of Providence bears a pair of scales—in this side He puts His people's trials, and in that He puts their consolations. When the scale of trial is nearly empty, you will always find the scale of consolation in nearly the same condition! ; and when the scale of trials is full, you will find the scale of consolation just as heavy.

When the black clouds gather most, the light is the more brightly revealed to us. When the night lowers and the tempest is coming on, the Heavenly Captain is always closest to His crew. It is a blessed thing, that when we are most cast down, then it is that we are most lifted up by the consolations of the Spirit. One reason is, because trials make more room for consolations. Great hearts can only be made by great troubles.

The spade of trouble digs the reservoir of comfort deeper, and makes more room for consolation. God comes into our heart—He finds it full—He begins to break our comforts and to make it empty; then there is more room for grace. The humbler a man lies, the more comfort he will always have because he will be more fitted to receive it. Another reason why we are most happy in our troubles is this—then we have the closest dealing with God.

When the barn is full, man can live without God: when the purse is bursting with gold, we try to do without so much prayer. But once take our gourds away, and we want our God; once cleanse the idols out of the house, then we are compelled to honor Jehovah.

"Out of the depths have I cried unto thee, O Lord." There is no cry so good as that which comes from the bottom of the mountains; no prayer half so hearty as that which comes up from the depths of the soul, through deep trials and afflictions. Hence they bring us to God, and we are happier; for nearness to God is happiness. Come, troubled believer, fret not over your heavy troubles, for they are the heralds of weighty mercies."
—Charles Spurgeon

December 10, 2003

Dear Family and Friends,

Last night, the kids and I stopped by Tim's room before bed. He'd been ill all week and seemed much worse. An ambulance was called, and Tim was taken next door to the ER. He had a fever of over 104, heart rate higher than 150, and his pupils were uneven.

The doctor said he has aspiration pneumonia. His white count was 18 (normal is 10). He is being given breathing treatments, oxygen, antibiotics, and fluids. The doctor said Tim might have a close shave here, but hopefully we will see an improvement in a few days. Tim already seems better to me. His pupils are still off, and I am waiting to see what the doctor says about that. The doctor said Tim's heart didn't sound right, so they will probably run some tests to see what is going on there. The last bad infection he had did some damage to his heart, and the doctor said he thought it sounded like there was fluid around it.

We finally got him settled at West Valley Hospital about 4 a.m. I'll keep you posted.

In His grip,
Carole

I stayed at the hospital with Tim, sleeping on a corner of his bed or propped up in a chair. Being overtired didn't help my thought life. I would catch the looks we were given by medical personnel and passersby and feel so terrible. Looks of pity. Sometimes, I felt like people were looking at me like, "Gosh, lady, why don't you let the poor guy go and quit prolonging his agony?"

I noticed something about myself during this time. I'm not an angry person, but sometimes I heard remarks or comments from people, and I felt they were insinuating that I wasn't doing the right things when it came to Tim's care. This filled me with absolute rage, but, fortunately, I kept my mouth shut. In reality, people were supportive, and no one was probably questioning my decisions. Deep down, I guess I felt guilty. I knew Tim's accident wasn't my fault, but because of the medical decisions I had made, I sometimes felt responsible for his current condition.

As time went on, I faced a daily battle of feelings and emotions. Rage, guilt, hopelessness, and depression—my emotions ran the gamut, and I cried out to God, one minute begging for help and the next minute accusing Him of deserting me. There were a few people that I could occasionally confide in, but most of the time I let God bear the brunt of my passions.

I threw tantrums before Him, acting just like a bratty, over-tired little two-year old who wasn't getting her way. Driving down the road to Tim's room, I would yell out loud in the car and cry and pound on the steering wheel. "I will never, never accept this! You must, must … you have to do something! Anything!

Don't leave Tim like this. My poor, poor baby! Please kill me. Give me cancer again. I don't care. Just get me out of here! I can't bear to watch Tim like this anymore! I can stand to see the pained looks on Becky's and Rachel's and Daniel's face when they look at their dad …"

I would go through a variation of this speech every couple of weeks for months. I can even remember telling the Lord once that I hated Him. I laugh at that now because it reminds me of a time when Rae was three years old, and I denied her something. She became angry with me, and when I turned my back to her, she stuck her tongue out at me. I don't know how, but I sensed it, caught her in the act, and to this day the girl lives in awe of me. She thinks I can read her mind.

Even though I felt like saying those things, I knew that even as I said them, I didn't mean them. I was merely acting like a wounded animal, lashing out at the kind hand that was stretched out to help me. God had trained us for more than 20 years to come to Him in good times, in bad times, until our response was nearly automatic. I knew that there was nowhere else to turn; I had nowhere else to go. Spent, I would crawl back into His everlasting arms and murmur, "I'm sorry, I didn't mean it. I love You."

I heard someone say once, "You Christians are all the same. God's just a crutch to you."

I replied, "Everybody needs a crutch to get through this world. What's yours? Escaping with alcohol or drugs? Empty man-made philosophies? My crutch is the great God of the universe!"

December 14, 2003
Dear Family and Friends,

Just a quick note to let you know that Tim is doing much better. His pneumonia is resolving, fever is coming down, and vitals are returning to what is normal for Tim. It sounds like he will be able to go back to Palm Valley in a couple of days. He still looks a little pale and tired, but there has been much improvement over the past couple of days.

I received a very nice letter from the Japanese woman who was driving the van that struck Tim. I am going to write her back and hopefully send her a Japanese Bible. Please pray that she will accept it, read it, and find comfort from God's word. She feels so terrible about Tim.

Today at church there was a children's choir production. All three of our kids were involved. Afterwards, we celebrated Becky's 17th birthday. It is hard, but life just continues on....

Peace,
Carole

Tim was finally moved back to Palm Valley. Right before he was discharged, another CT scan was done. The scan didn't show any new changes and the doctor said everything was chronic (severe brain injury, enlarged but stable ventricles, encephalomalacia, brain atrophy, etc.). He again stated Tim's prognosis and added that he thought Tim would be a quadriplegic. I said, "Well, that's news to me."

I told him that I didn't totally agree with that assessment. My understanding of paralysis was no movement and no feeling, and Tim could feel pain everywhere. His right arm probably had some paralysis, but he moved his other arm. As for his legs, he didn't move them, but he could feel pain in them, and we saw some very slight movements once in a while. So, the doctor explained that he felt Tim would never regain control over his muscle movements.

I often wondered what the doctors expected me to do with their prognosis. I wondered if they expected us to quit talking to Tim, reading to him, singing to him. I wondered if they expected us to stop loving him. They acted like we should just give up and walk away, and while I believed that I had surrendered Tim's future to God to do whatever He deemed best, I wouldn't stop acting like he was valuable to us even though he was severely disabled.

As I looked around at the world, I saw God working and answering prayer. Saddam Hussein had just been caught! I didn't know why God remained silent about Tim. But I knew He was listening. There were days when I gave Him a very passionate earful. It felt good to vent, and He had the biggest shoulders to cry on. And besides, He already knew what I was thinking, so I might as well fess up and let Him have it.

But afterwards, I always felt so lousy, so I would start going down my list of truths. I started thanking Him for everything I could think of. The first thing I thanked Him for was eternal life and the hope of heaven. A lot of the time, I didn't even need to go past that one. It was so huge, and the thought of it actually made me feel euphoric. I didn't stop ticking off truths until I quit feeling lousy.

19

"Lord, You've Got Some Explaining to Do!"

December 25, 2003

Merry Christmas

I hope you had a very special Christmas day. We had such a nice day with my folks. There were a couple of rough moments. Yesterday, Dan was a bit grumpy and said he didn't feel very good. I knew he had been so hoping that Tim would be better by today, and I wondered if his behavior had anything to do with how he was feeling. This morning, he got up and I went after my usual morning hug and kiss, and he just held onto me for the longest time. We just stood there snuggling, and he finally said, "I wish Daddy was home."

Then he looked up at me and said, "I just don't get it. I know you guys are always saying that there is a purpose in everything, but if Daddy goes to heaven now, I just don't see what the purpose of that could be."

I said, "I don't see the purpose either, and I don't understand this at all. And yet, the Bible says there is a reason. We may never understand until we're in heaven, too, but someday we will see and understand why this was allowed to happen."

I wish I had answers for him. Then Becky did the sweetest thing. She found the photos from our wedding and put them in a beautiful album as a Christmas present for Tim and me. That is something that I have been meaning to do for 20 years. It's hard to look at all those pictures, though.

I know this is going to sound silly because God doesn't operate like this. Still, sometimes I think if I just hit on the right thing in prayer that maybe He will be moved to act. I pray scripture to Him because I know He can't go against His own word, and today I felt like I really had Him on a certain point. I have been so concerned about Daniel (all the kids really, but Dan is the youngest and the least grounded in his *faith)—I know he tries to understand what is happening and to have faith, but this is inexplicable and hard even for an adult to comprehend and deal with.*

I can't imagine how it must be for him. Anyway, a scripture came to mind after my conversation with Daniel (Matt. 18:6 "... but whoever causes one of these little ones who believe in Me to stumble, it would be better for him to have a heavy millstone hung around his neck and to be drowned in the depth of the sea.")

Aha! I got You on this point. I said, "Lord, You just can't allow Dan's faith to be tested until it is destroyed. That would be causing him to stumble! I want You to act, to do something. I can explain Tim's recovery or even partial recovery to Daniel. I can even explain Daddy going home to be with You. But I simply do not have the words to explain to Daniel that his dad will never wake up and that he will remain as he is forever. I can talk to Becky and Rachel about it—and that is extremely painful and difficult—but I just can't say that to Daniel. I think it would be too much for him to bear. I am afraid he will become angry with You and hate You.

"Sometimes, when I am soooooo frustrated over what has happened to Tim, I feel absolute rage and want to scream and hit things, and I'm (supposedly) a mature adult. What is my little boy going to do? I know that You are able to keep our feet from slipping (Psalm 121), and maybe I am underestimating both Dan and You, but at what point does this become too much to bear?

"When we began home schooling the kids, Tim and I had one goal only. We decided that it didn't matter to us if our kids turned out to be as dumb as stumps. All we wanted was for them to love You and to follow You. If they grew up to love the You with all their hearts, then we would feel that we had done our job right. Lord, Daniel trusts You! Don't let him down. Let Daniel's faith stand firm. Don't give him too much to handle. Don't let your little one stumble."

I hope and pray that you made some wonderful memories today. Our last two Christmases have been merry, although unusual. Unforgettable for sure. One of my most unforgettable Christmases was the year Dan was born. I remember sitting in the Christmas Eve service holding our two-month-old baby boy.

Brother Vince D. began to talk about the incarnation. He spoke of Mary lovingly holding her newborn baby boy with his chubby, pink little hands and tiny little feet. Hands and feet that were created for the sole purpose of being pierced for us. I sat there looking down at Dan's tiny little hands, and I thought how much I would grieve if anything were to happen to him. I marveled at God's great love toward us. Love that would motivate Him to endure the pain of seeing His beloved Son suffer on our behalf.

Long lay the world, in sin and error pining,
Till He appeared, and the soul felt its worth.
A thrill of hope, the weary world rejoices,
For yonder breaks a new and glorious morn.
Fall on your knees! O hear the angel voices!
O night divine! O night, when Christ was born.
O night divine! O night, O Holy night.
—Placide Cappeau

Merry Christmas,
Carole and the Kids

Immobility was causing a lot of problems for Tim. He had pressure sores and constantly had to be turned to keep his weight off of them. He had edema in both legs. Other issues included: the hole where his tracheostomy used to be not completely healing. He had thrush and still struggled with UTIs. It seemed like there was always some problem to be dealt with.

I stopped by one warm January day to sit with Tim, and the nurses had opened the windows of his room. There was sunlight, fresh air, and bird sounds. Maybe it was the different light in the room, but Tim looked really pale and had dark circles under his eyes. One of the nurses speculated that Tim was getting depressed over his condition and that that was why he wasn't responsive anymore. I had no idea how we would know that for sure. I suspected it was due to his physical condition. Since December 1, I could pretty much count Tim's "good" days (days where he seems to be feeling well) on one hand.

I began to notice I felt good on the days Tim seemed to be feeling good, and when he was struggling or sick, I felt pretty low. The kids were keeping busy. It was amazing to me how we humans adjusted to whatever circumstances we found ourselves in. You really weren't given a choice. You just kept getting up every day and time went by. It had been almost six months since Tim's accident.

January 11, 2004

Dear Family and Friends,
Looking back over the past few months, I have seen the body of Christ provoked into action and made more ready for the Lord's coming. I have seen the love and grace of God, once again, never fail. I have learned that surrendering, while sounding like a weak thing to do, is actually a very, very strenuous, difficult thing to do. I've become

aware that I love Tim, and even myself, probably more than I love the Lord, and my prayer lately is to love Christ above all else. Then I know I will be all right with whatever He decides. I am really trying to comprehend and live the verses in the Bible that talk about dying to ourselves.

Someone once said, "It is the life of self which causes us pain; that which is dead does not suffer." I realize that on the days that I am arguing with God about my circumstances, telling Him this is too hard, it hurts too much, that it's my selfish self getting in the way again. Galations 2:20 says, "I have been crucified with Christ; and it is no longer I who live, but Christ lives in me; and the life which I now live in the flesh I live by faith in the Son of God, who loved me and gave Himself up for me."

It's a daily (all day) thing, trying to be obedient and surrendered to the will of God when you don't exactly like your circumstances. Between that and badgering the Lord in prayer constantly, I am kept pretty busy—and out of trouble! Remember the night Christ was arrested, He said, "My Father, if it is possible, let this cup pass from Me, yet not as I will, but as You will. He went away again a second time and prayed, saying, "My Father, if this cannot pass away unless I drink it, Your will be done." And He left them again, and went away and prayed a third time, saying the same thing once more.

I figure if the Lord (who knew exactly what lay ahead, how long the ordeal would last, and the outcome) prayed that way, then it is OK for me (the puny human who doesn't have a clue about what's happening) to pray that way. Father, change Your mind! Think of another way! But, Your will be done, not mine.

By the way, Happy New Year. Wonder what this year has in store for all of us?

Peace,
Carole

We were receiving a lot of positive feedback about the Web site. Several people mentioned that they thought I should write a book someday. I began to realize that sharing my heart and our lives was becoming a ministry to others. I began hearing from complete strangers, telling me how much our family meant to them. It was incredible.

Looking back on this time, I can see now that each subsequent infection that Tim had took a bit more out of him. I, too, began to realize that many of the things Tim did that we thought were responses were merely reflexive actions. Very, very rarely, he would follow a command, but most of the time his movements and motions were random, and he did them whether we were around or not. I remember walking quietly into his room and standing at the threshold observing his behavior.

Sometimes, you could practically set your watch by his movements. He seemed to cycle through them, and it was so pitiful and disheartening to see. Confused, I asked Tim's doctor how he could seemingly respond one time and then not again for the next several days. He said Tim probably slipped into minimal consciousness once in a while, but 98 percent of the time he was comatose.

Minimal consciousness still isn't conscious, though. I tried to describe it to the kids this way: The first thing that I remember after one of my surgeries was waking up in my hospital room. But, evidently, the surgical team had actually brought me out of the anesthesia in the operating room. They had talked to me and told me to cough and open my eyes, and I had obeyed them. Yet, I don't recall that at all. I was only minimally conscious.

So, Tim infrequently responded to our commands, but that didn't mean that he realized he was doing it. That also meant that he probably didn't realize that the kids and I were there with him. How very sad.

20

"To Have and To Hold"

January 25, 2004

> *"Pain is the plow that tears up our hearts*
> *to make us open to truth."*
> —Eberhard Arnold

Dear Family and Friends,

I realize that my updates are few and far between these days—the reason being that there hasn't been any change in Tim's condition recently.

It has now been six months since Tim was injured. At this point, the prayers of my family have changed somewhat as we watch Tim struggle day after day. We ask the Lord to either wake Tim or take Tim. Have we stopped believing that God can miraculously heal Tim? Absolutely not. The Bible says that nothing is too hard for God. Look at His track record: creates the universe in six days, parts the sea, raises the dead, heals the blind and lame, just to name a few. How hard could it be to wake a guy from a coma?

Do I believe that God will heal Tim miraculously? I really do not know, and this is my struggle. Some days I think we just need to wait a bit longer for an answer to our prayers, and other days, I think God has answered us with a big, fat "No." Since I don't know the answer, I simply act each day on the knowledge that I do have.

I know that the only thing Tim loves above his family is the Lord. If he can't be with his family, he would rather be with the Lord. I know, now, for a Christian there can be such a thing as a "fate worse than death." I know Tim will continue to suffer on a daily basis if he doesn't wake up. So I pray for two possible solutions. "Father, wake Tim or take Tim."

There is a third possiblilty—Tim remains in the state he is in right now.

As I dwell on that scenario, my heart starts to sink at the ramifications for Tim, the kids, and myself. But always, always when I think about this third possibility, I am filled with confidence in the Lord's character, and I know without a doubt that He will do the right thing. Will not the Judge of all the earth do what is right? (Genesis 18:25)

I got an e-mail today from my good friend, Michiko, in Japan. I wanted to paste a little of her letter on this update for you to read. She refers to "Sachiko" in her e-mail—that is the Japanese lady who was driving the van that hit Tim:

I sent letter and Bible and the book to Sachiko yesterday, and she called me tonight. She thanked me for translating your letter for her, and she said she will read the Bible! She felt bad about Tim's condition and that she was thankful for your kind words towards her. I told my boys about the call (they were reading books on my bed), and we prayed right away that Sachiko will open her heart and believe in Jesus.

And let me tell you what happened yesterday when I went to the post office in my town to mail the letter and the Bible. A few months ago when we had Youth Rally in our church, I sent off about 100 applications to the students who have been to our past three Youth Rallies. I told the lady at the window at the post office that I need a receipt. She gave me the receipt, and then she asked me why I was sending all these letters. I told her about the church and Youth Rally. She asked me where the church is located at in Misawa. I told her where and I invited her to church.

Well, she never came to church. Anyway, when I went yesterday, she was at the window, and as usual smile nicely, and we said hi to each other. I asked her if I could send the Bible registered because I wanted to make sure that it got to her. She said there is a cheaper way to send small packages and just as secure as registered, and it only takes a day or two for delivery. She was just very helpful and nice. She helped me to write the address in the right place since this used a special envelope and when we were about to be done, she asked me if I was sending a Bible.

I was kind a surprised just because she was right, and I told her "Yes, I was." Then she tells me that she is married to an American Air Force guy, and he is in Korea for a year (he will be back this fall, she said) but he told her that when he comes back, he wants to go to church and asked her to find a church. I thought to myself "Oh my ... I know God's plan is perfect, but it is full of surprises sometimes."

I can say with all honesty that I will never, on this earth at least, be able to thank God for what has happened to Tim. It is just too sad, too terrible. But, I am to the point that I can thank God for how He is using this situation. So many people, I have been told, have been impacted by what has happened to my family. I am amazed and encouraged. Amazed because as I watch God bring some beautiful things out of the ashes of our lives, as always He proves that He knows what He is doing. I am encour-

aged because it seems that what has happened to us fits into something beyond the scope of our little lives—it helps to know that what you are going through isn't just a great big, terrible, purposeless, random mistake.

I am reminded of what Paul said when he was in prison in Philippi, "Now, I want you to know, brethren, that my circumstances have turned out for the greater progress of the gospel ... and in this I rejoice." (Phil 1:12, 18) Granted, Tim hasn't been imprisoned for sharing his faith, but, as a part of God's greater plan, he is imprisoned in a broken body on this cursed and rebellious planet. Yet, his circumstances are making lots of people re-evaluate their lives and priorities. His circumstances are making people realize that life is fragile and brief, and because of that, they are motivated to live with purpose. People are being drawn to the Lord. I can rejoice in this and Tim would, too.

I will be facing some really major decisions and projects in the next few weeks and months. I would appreciate prayer for wisdom.

You've heard the saying "paralyzed with fear?" Well, sometimes I feel paralyzed with ignorance. To all my girlfriends out there ... if you are as dependent on your hubby as I was, watch out! I pray that nothing like this will ever happen to you, but if it does, you will probably feel as helpless as I did. Please take some time to sit down with your husband and find out where everything is. Educate yourself!

When Tim's widowed grandma was here visiting, we sat in the car at the gas station one day laughing at ourselves. Both of us had always let our hubbies fill up the car. So, when we had to start going to the gas station by ourselves, we had trouble figuring out how to run those new-fangled pumps! Talk about feeling dumb. Becky can pump gas, she's learning to balance the checkbook, and she will know how to do taxes in a few weeks—all because of what I have gone through. Fortunately, I am surrounded by some sharp folks who don't mind my stupid questions (I hope), and I am a fast learner.

God bless you.

February 1, 2004

"Faith is simply trusting in God when life gives you reason not to."
—Corrie Ten Boom

Dear Family and Friends,

Just a quick report on Tim. On Monday, Becky and I pushed Tim to the medical office building next door for his appointment with the ENT doctor. We had to borrow a wheelchair because Tim's is still on order. It was a beautiful day, but a bit chilly, so we bundled Tim up with blankets, stuck a stocking cap on his head, put some sunglasses on him and started rolling him down the hall. We got to the outer door, and one of Tim's former nurses inquired how he was doing and where we were going with him. She laughed as we told her that we were busting Tim out. The walk to the doctor only took about three minutes. You should have seen the way people looked at us. Tim is still Tim to me, and I guess I don't realize how his condition looks to other people.

The ENT said Tim would require surgery to completely close the trachea hole. I told him that I didn't want to subject Tim to any surgery that could be avoided. He said the opening wasn't affecting his oxygen intake and that we could leave everything as is. By the time we got Tim "home," he was pretty tired. I don't know if he was aware that he was outside or somewhere different. All I know is that everything is pretty hard on him.

Oh, I am in the process of buying a house. It is finally time, for several reasons that I won't go into. But, I made an offer, and it has been accepted. Hopefully, we'll close next month. Our house is in the same subdivision and it backs up to the lake, just like where we live now. It is a bit more spacious, and there is a room that could be used for Tim and his equipment if he is able to come home.

The evening that I made the offer, I didn't sleep at all. I tossed and turned all night, wondering what Tim would have done. I'm still second guessing myself but doing the best that I can. It's like Becky said the other night, "Mom, it's not like there's a handbook for you to follow." So, I'm just winging it as I go. Every once in a while, I turn to the kids and say, "Hey, we're doing OK, aren't we? The family hasn't fallen apart (it has just been maimed)—wouldn't your dad be proud of us?" I think he would be amazed.

Love,
Carole and Kids

February 6, 2004

Dear Family and Friends,

Had to laugh the other day … Rae and I were driving home from her martial arts class one evening last week and as we pulled up to a red light, I thought I heard a noise *coming from under the hood of the car. I thought to myself, "Hmm, that's a new sound." Over the next day or two, the sound became more noticeable, and I thought I remembered hearing a similar sound in our old van a few years ago. It was kind of a gravely sound.*

Tim had determined that the water pump was shot and replaced it. Long story short, I took the car to a mechanic friend and said I thought my water pump was going out. Lo and behold, it was! What made me laugh was the fact that I even had a clue as to what was wrong with the car (thank you, Lord). My dad taught me how to pump gas, check the oil and transmission fluid, and how to change a tire when I was a teenager (all of which Tim has been doing for me for 20 years), and that is pretty much the extent of my knowledge of cars.

Maybe I will write a handbook after all ... I could call it "The Helpless Home-maker Survival Handbook" and include some of the things I have had to learn during the past six months. I was really content until my little bubble of life was burst. At first, I was so sad and so scared. I wanted to crawl into bed, pull the covers over my head, and cry until it all went away. After that, I seethed with resentment over the demands that were suddenly placed on me.

"This isn't my job! Why do I have to deal with this? I am not equipped to handle all of this!" Then came the point of surrender—which took quite a while. I just simply quit arguing with God and said, "Not my will, but Thine." I have to say that every single day, but it has made such a difference. I don't feel quite as much pressure, although there is still loads to do. I still feel a little fearful when I think about the future, and I struggle with guilt over not being with Tim 24/7, or being with the kids 24/7 ... but you can only spread one person so thin.

I daily thank God for His grace, which is indeed sufficient. I thank God for His strength. I constantly think about 2 Cor. 3:4, and 4:7, "Not that we are adequate in ourselves to consider anything as coming from ourselves, but our adequacy is from God ... But we have this treasure in earthen vessels, so that the surpassing greatness of the power will be of God and not from ourselves."

I am just a jar of clay, or maybe even a very cracked pot—beaten up and quite battered—but because of God's personal presence in our lives, we can say with Paul, "we are afflicted in every way, but not crushed; perplexed, but not despairing; persecuted, but not forsaken; struck down, but not destroyed."

If you see anything going right in the kids and me, we will be the first to tell you it is all Christ—you are seeing Him through the cracks in our jars of clay. I am so thankful to Him because without Him, I would be so lost. The kids look to God as their dad now, and as far as I'm concerned, He's my provider, defender, protector, just like Tim used to be. We keep telling Him, "We're your problem now!" We used to be Tim's!

I guess everything is going OK with the house. The appraisal is supposed to be done. The inspection is Monday. Found out yesterday that no termites have squatter's rights at the new place, so that's a relief. No glitches yet. I keep getting a lot of papers in the mail, and I am not exactly sure what they are, but help is just a phone call away. I also just found out that I need to start the paperwork for Tim's retirement—and I have yet to start on our taxes! I'm buried in paperwork—that's the bad news. But, the good news is, God is still in control, and my checkbook balanced (to the penny) again this month.

Total Consecration

"If you ask how you may know that you have truly consecrated yourself to Him, I reply, observe every indication of His will concerning you, no matter how trivial, and see whether you at once close in with that will. Lay down this principle as law—God does nothing arbitrarily. If He takes away your health, for instance, it is because He has some reason for doing so; and this is true of everything you value; and if you have real faith in Him, you will not insist on knowing the reason.

If you find, in the course of daily events, that your self-consecration revolts at His will—do not be discouraged, but fly to your Savior and stay in His presence till you obtain the spirit in which He cried in His hour of anguish, "Father, if thou be willing, remove this cup from me: nevertheless not my will, but Thine, be done." Luke 22:42.

Every time you do this it will be easier to do it; every such consent to suffer will bring you nearer and nearer to Him; and in this nearness to Him you will find such peace, such blessed, sweet peace as will make your life infinitely happy, no matter what may be its mere outside conditions. Just think of the honor and the joy of having your will one with the Divine will and so becoming changed into Christ's image from glory to glory!"

—Elizabeth Prentiss

In His Grip,
Carole and the kids

21

"For Richer, For Poorer"

In early March, we moved into our new home. Moving day was one of the most encouraging days of our lives. We were moved "locust style," as our friend Jim put it. Our church family descended on our old place like a swarm of locusts—every last thing was picked up and carried off to the new place. Not only that, but the old house was cleaned and the new house all set up by 3 p.m. The furniture was placed and put together, audio/video equipment hooked up, shelves lined, books unpacked, dishes put away, beds made, lawn mowed, weeds pulled … you get the idea. Desert Springs and my folks went way beyond the call of duty.

March 14, 2004

> *"Great is the Lord and most worthy of praise;*
> *His greatness no one can fathom."*
> *Psalm 145: 3*

Dear Family and Friends,

It has been quite a while since I have been able to write anything encouraging regarding Tim's condition. However, over the past few weeks, we have been noticing a few new responses. But I hesitated to write about them because the doctors have said all along that Tim might be able to follow a few commands. I think, too, that the kids and I are almost afraid to get excited for fear of being let down or disappointed. So, we just observe and wonder.

It actually started a few weeks ago; Tim shut his eyes when Mom asked him to. Over the next few days and weeks, he began to follow this command nearly every time he was asked. The interesting thing about it was that his response was immediate. There was no delay in responding, whereas before, his responses sometimes took 30–45 seconds. I began asking him to let go of my hand and move it away, rather than squeezing or gripping my hand, which is sometimes reflexive for Tim. He seemed to be getting this response down, too.

When I arrived Friday morning, he had his eyes wide open and seemed pretty relaxed, but I figured he needed rest as he'd been sick recently, so I read to him a little, gave him a shave, and just sat with him.

A bit later, Lisa (nurse's aide) came in to check on Tim and as she said, "Hi, Tim!"—his eyebrows shot up. I laughed and said, "Hey, he knows your voice!" I have seen him do that when we walk in, too, lately. Realizing that we might have a brief window of opportunity, I asked him to raise his eyebrows again. He did—that is the first time he has done that for me. Not only that, but he followed that command three times in a row. Then I asked him to stick out his tongue. I had seen him stick out his tongue the week before, not as a result of a command, but just something new his body could do, so I have been asking him and asking him to stick out his tongue for me since then and he hasn't been able to.

Well, as soon as I asked him to stick out his tongue, he did! He needed a little rest and then was able to follow that command again. He began moving his mouth in a new way, so I asked him if he was trying to say something or smile. He smiled with the left side of his mouth. I said, "Tim, you smiled! Can you do it again?" He smiled the same way. The third time I asked him, he gave me a full smile. (Yes, I was bawling by this time.)

He did a couple of other things on cue, and then I started to try to get a "yes" or "no" response from him. We weren't having any luck there, so I finally said, "Tim, can you do something to communicate? Move something? Blink? Anything?" I had been holding his hand and as soon as I asked him that he very firmly, deliberately squeezed my hand three times in a row! I was on the phone to the kids, my mom, out in the hall telling all the nurses and anyone else who would listen! By this time, Tim was pretty tired, so I said I would come back later with the kids.

When I got home, it was kind of hard to remain calm. We don't know what this sudden flurry of activity means, but after seeing very little over the past few months, we are definitely encouraged. I am especially encouraged because while the doctors have said Tim will be able to follow commands, they have also said he will not be able to communicate. I believe that Tim definitely communicated with me for the very first time in nearly eight months.

I wish I could say that Tim's responses have been as dramatic since then, but he hasn't been feeling very well, and we don't like to pester him when he is in pain. Still, when the kids and I went back to his room, even though Tim was not feeling well, he tried so hard to do what we asked. He lifted his eyebrows, stuck out his tongue, and moved his arm. Mom said when she stopped by, he was tired, but when she asked Tim *to smile, he sighed and reluctantly smiled. We could just imagine him joking, "What am I? A performing animal? Leave me alone!"*

Thanks for continuing to pray for Tim. You are so faithful! And Lord, so are You. The Lord is faithful to all His promises and loving toward all He has made. The Lord upholds all those who fall and lifts up all who are bowed down. The Lord is near to all who call on Him, to all who call on Him in truth. He fulfills the desires of those who fear Him; He hears their cry and saves them."
Psalm 145: 13,14,18,19

Love,
Carole and the kids

What a difference a day makes. One minute you're on top of the world, and the next, you're in the valley of the shadow. The very next day, I walked into Tim's room, certain that we had turned a corner in his recovery. But something was very wrong and within minutes, Tim began having grand mal seizures and was rushed to the hospital.

I began to notice a pattern at the various emergency rooms we had frequented in the past couple of months. Each time the doctors came in to evaluate Tim, they always asked me if I wanted Tim to receive treatment and if I wanted him resuscitated should his heart stop. I said, "No way," to the resuscitation and "absolutely" to the treatment. I did say that their treatment didn't have to be really, really aggressive. If God was intent on taking Tim, no one was to thwart that—not that I or anyone could do that anyway.

Not to complain, because Tim was always well cared for and people were usually great … But I began to notice that once you placed someone in the hospital, you powered up a gigantic machine that was difficult to turn off. Things that are done "in the name of healing" are sometimes just done to cover somebody's fanny and protect them from a potential lawsuit. And things are done as long as the insurance company agrees with it. I had noticed that with the many therapists we dealt with. As long as our insurance company was still paying for treatment, Tim seemed to be making progress. But every time the insurance company stopped paying, it was, "I'm sorry Mrs. Jones, but we can't continue if Tim isn't progressing." I wasn't sure which was more discouraging—the no-hope neurosurgeons or the false-hope therapists. I really began to dislike taking Tim to the hospital because he always seemed to be subjected to much, much more than was necessary to help him.

The seizures were pretty bad, but the docs got them stopped and controlled with medication. Most likely, the seizures were due to his original brain injury. The neurologist said it wasn't all that uncommon for seizures to start, even at this late date. The injury and resulting atrophy of the brain produced a "focus" point allowing seizures a place to begin. Tim was also slightly septic due to his chronic UTI.

He was finally discharged from the hospital ten days later. We placed him at Sunbridge Estrella Rehab and Care in Avondale. Palm Valley was unable to provide the staff to give Tim his intravenous antibiotics every six hours, so we had to find another place.

Sunbridge was very nice and as close to our home as Palm Valley. We liked the staff, and the rooms and the facility in general. It was encouraging to walk into Tim's room and see his nurse's aide, Lupe, kindly talking to Tim as she got him ready for the day. I told her how much I appreciated the way she treated him. It turned out that their rates were lower, too, which helped me out a lot.

Up to this point, we still had Tim's income as well as Social Security to live on, but Tim's care was catastrophically expensive and our savings were dwindling. I truly expected to get the full three-pronged Job-like trial—the personal hit (cancer), the family hit (Tim), and the financial hit. But, the financial loss never materialized. I sat daily at my desk, paying bill after bill, always coming to the end of our money before I came to the end of the stack. At that point, I would put my head in my hands and pray, "Lord, I'm a thousand dollars (or two thousand, or three thousand or more) short again this month." It seemed that each month that we came up lacking, I would walk to our mailbox and find a gift from someone that matched the exact amount of debt that we owed. From my lips to God's ear.

Every time Tim got sick and was hospitalized, it set him back further. And there was never another "golden" day again.

22

"To Love and To Cherish"

Day after day, life was the same. Tim was either well or he was sick, but other than that, his condition didn't change. I went to see him every day, usually twice a day, and I washed him, shaved him, combed his hair, gave him a haircut when needed, and then I sat with him. I'd tell him about the kids' doings, read to him, but mainly I just crawled up on his bed and held his hand or put my arms around him and laid my head on his chest.

I stayed overnight in his room when he was sick. I helped the nurses change him and dress him. I marveled at how our relationship had changed. Tim had always taken care of me, and yes, I had babied him, too, like a lover would. But now, it was as if I had become his mother.

Our kids were living a dual life. They loved and missed their dad, but it had been almost a year and life had gone on. I didn't want life to stop for them. They were young. Their whole lives were ahead of them. They seemed like well-adjusted, happy kids at home, at church, with their friends. But a change would come over them as we drove up to Sunbridge. They became quiet and distant and depressed and walked down the long hallway to their dad's room looking at the ground.

Even though Sunbridge was a nice facility, my kids still saw shocking things from time to time. I tried to come up with things for them to do with their dad. I said they could read to him or sing, and they would try, but pretty soon their voices would trail off, and they would be choked up with tears. I could relate because often as I sat with Tim and tried to talk to him, I would fight back my own tears. Most often, they would sit and read and not interact with Tim very much. I understood why. Even though they knew that their dad couldn't help it, they felt rejected by him. He never looked at them; he never talked to them or responded to them. Rae blurted out tearfully one day, "It just doesn't seem like my dad!"

People who stopped by to visit Tim would often tell us how much Tim had responded to them. Even though we knew that most of the time Tim's responses were being misinterpreted, we never said anything, but that made the kids feel even worse.

"Everyone keeps saying daddy responds to them. How come he never responds to me?"

I would patiently explain that those well-meaning folks might have been mistaken. I told them, too, that everyone loved their dad and it meant a lot to them to feel like they had a special moment with him.

I finally said to them one day, "I don't think it is good for you to visit your dad everyday." They looked at me with shock and began to protest, "No, Mommy, we're sorry that we're not more happy there. It is just so sad to see him like this. We'll act better ..."

I said, "You don't have to feel guilty about this. This is my decision, and I am doing what I think is best for you. You can visit your dad any time you want, but I want you to take a break. It looks like your dad could be like this for a real long time, but I know that he would want you to keep on living. He wants you to grow up and be happy. He knows that you love him. But you need to take a break from Sunbridge."

The kids still visited their dad frequently, but not every day.

◆　　　◆　　　◆

In May, Tim's leave ran out and his employment with the Department of Defense ended. I was so thankful that we were given so much time to see what would happen with his condition. Things would get "interesting" financially, but I'd just had a crash course in remaining calm. Like the great missionary Hudson Taylor, I had an opportunity to see what God could do.

I sat down one night and, just for kicks, added up all the paid medical bills from the first of the year. I was stunned at the total, and completely in awe of the Lord's provision. It reminded me of our earlier, leaner years together when Tim supported our family on Guam with just his teacher's salary.

We always got to the end of the year with the bills paid and no debt, but we really didn't understand how that had happened. We were both pretty good at math, but two plus two didn't equal four in our budget. It was more like two plus two equals eight. Another of the Lord's specialties—multiplying fish and loaves.

I thanked God every single day for His faithfulness in providing for Tim and me and the kids. I was also thankful for Tim's wacky sense of humor, which was genetically transmitted to all three of our kids. The kids and I had been discussing our situation before prayer time one evening and we finally decided that if things got really tight, we'd just start visiting all the relatives that we'd never visited or imposed upon before!

As the months progressed, God worked on my heart. For some reason, in my heart and in my mind, the anniversary of Tim's accident became my D-day for God. I felt that if God didn't move by then, He wasn't planning on moving.

I had been telling Him all along that there were two possible scenarios that I would accept from Him. One was that Tim could get all better or even some better. It would be fine with me if he would just wake up enough to know us. I didn't mind taking care of him if he was disabled for the rest of his life. I had no life to get back to once this was "all over." Tim was my life. I loved him, probably even more than ever before, and he needed me.

The second scenario was that God would take Tim to heaven. I wouldn't even have minded if He let me tag along! Heaven was such an attractive option at this point. There was a third scenario—that God allowed Tim to stay exactly as he was.

Unacceptable, but definitely a possibility. I had heard about the circus revolving around Terry Schiavo in Florida. Thirteen years. How awful for everyone involved.

When I first heard that her husband had become involved with another woman and even fathered children, I was so disgusted. But, then I got to thinking … what would I be like after so long? Thirteen years from now, how would I act? Would I become unfaithful to Tim? I didn't even want to know the answer to those questions.

Somewhere along the way, I gave up. I gave up my life. I gave up Tim's life. I told the Lord that whatever He planned to do was OK with me. Tim's doctor had told me that if he survived the first year, that he had a good chance of surviving for a very long time. When I asked, "How long?" he had said, "Oh, he could go on like this for twenty or thirty years."

I couldn't speak for several minutes after that. When I could speak, I spoke to the Lord. "You win. If this is going to be our life from now on, show me how to live like this, because I really don't know how. I do not know how to be joyful in the midst of this. And, I have needs. Either take them away or meet them. I'm through telling You what You can and can't do with my life."

God began to answer that prayer in ways that I never dreamed. Pastor Steve and Tami asked us out for ice cream one afternoon, and as we sat there, Steve asked me to take on the Awana program at our church. Times had really changed. Awana is a huge program, and if he had asked me to do that a year ago I would have run away screaming. But, the thought immediately came into my mind, "That ought to be a piece of cake compared to what I've been handling this past year!" So, I agreed to do it.

What a blessing! I was in way over my head with this challenge and it completely consumed and distracted me. Not only that, but I loved working with the kids and the Awana staff. I felt like my life had some purpose again. Becky, Rachel, and Daniel were all involved, as well, and I loved serving with them. We began to see that as we lost ourselves in serving God and others, real joy returned to our lives.

June 13, 2004

> *"I call as my heart grows faint;*
> *lead me to the rock that is higher than I."*
> *Psalm 61:2*

Dear Family and Friends,

You know, we're a month away from the one-year anniversary of Tim's accident, and I know from all of my reading that the likelihood of someone coming out of a vegetative state at this point is nil. I think it is OK to say this—the kids and I know Dad isn't going to get better here on earth. For whatever His reasons, God turned down our request. I have really struggled with the disappointment of it all, and I just didn't know what to say to all of you who have hoped and prayed as diligently as my family has.

Even in the midst of struggling with this though, God is so loving and patient. He stirred up a good friend of ours to call me all the way from Japan just to ask how I was doing. And he really, really meant "How are you?" so I told him—and felt much better, thank you very much! There are so many things that I feel like I can only say to God because I feel that He is the only one who can hear it all and still love and accept me. So, I am very grateful for Don's listening ear.

Then, this dear friend sent me a powerful book called Shattered Dreams, *by Larry Crabb. It was 200 pages long, and I am soooooo busy that I hardly have time to read recipes, let alone an entire book. But, I devoured it in less than three days, even taking it with me in the car and reading it at stoplights. Here's the premise of the book:*

1. God wants to bless you. He gets a kick out of making His children happy. We were created for happiness and, therefore, our souls long for whatever we think will provide the greatest possible pleasure.

2. The deepest pleasure (highest blessing) we're capable of experiencing is a direct encounter with God. He does us the most good by seeing to it that we seek an encounter with Him with more energy than we seek anything else. But we almost always mistake lesser pleasures for this greatest pleasure and live our lives chasing after them. We're not in touch with our appetite for God.

3. So the Holy Spirit awakens that appetite. He uses the pain of shattered dreams to help us discover our desire for God, to help us begin dreaming the highest dream. Shattered dreams are not accidents of fate. They are ordained opportunities for the Spirit first to awaken and then satisfy our highest dream.

4. The problem is that we don't believe this idea is true. We assent to it in our heads. But we don't feel it in our hearts.

(from Shattered Dreams, *by Larry Crabb)*

The book really spoke to my heart, so much so that as I began reading it, I actually said out loud, "Who is this guy and how did he get inside my head?" I had been walking around for a month praying, "OK, Lord, what do you want from me? What am I supposed to do now?" and I felt like that prayer was answered as I finished reading.

So, today I pray for God to be merciful to Tim, that as soon as He sees fit that He would set Tim free from being imprisoned in his broken body and mind. And I ask Him to become my greatest desire—I'm not there yet, but I know that is where I need to be (we all do). Otherwise, I will crave the pleasures and blessings that I experienced when my family was intact and be forever depressed, disappointed, and discouraged.

> *"Oh, Great Shepherd, add to Your mercies this one other—*
> *a heart to love You more truly as I ought."*
> —Charles Spurgeon

Some days, I was so fatigued that I fell asleep at stoplights. I started to wonder if I shouldn't go out and get one of those bumper stickers that said, "If you don't like my driving, then stay off the sidewalk!"

Life was crazy and hectic, and it was easy to get caught up in all the details of things that had to be done. Becky and I were in Walmart one morning getting our weekly groceries. Being coupon clippers and sale shoppers we decided to take a look at the clearance rack. Becky pulled out a shirt and said, "Mom, you've got to get this." The shirt had a cartoonish drawing of a woman "on the edge"—actually, this woman looked like she'd gotten to "the edge" and just kept right on going. Her eyes were bugging out and her hair was standing on end and she was hollering, "It's been 'fun,' but I have to SCREAM NOW!" We laughed until tears came to our eyes, and I said to Becky, "That's me, that's my life."

"If only I knew where to find Him!" Job 23:3
"In Job's uttermost extremity he cried after the Lord. The longing desire of an afflicted
child of God is once more to see his Father's face. His first prayer is not 'O, that I
might be healed of the disease which now festers in every part of my body!' nor even 'O,
that I might see my children restored from the jaws of the grave, and my property once
more brought from the hand of the spoiler!'
but the first and uppermost cry is,
'O, that I knew where I might find Him, who is my God!
That I might come even to His seat!'
God's children run home when the storm comes on ... he bids farewell to earthborn
hopes, and cries, 'If only I knew where to find Him!' Nothing teaches us so much the
preciousness of the Creator, as when we learn the emptiness of all besides. Turning
away with bitter scorn from earth's hives, where we find no honey, but many sharp
stings, we rejoice in Him whose faithful word is sweeter than honey or the honeycomb.
In every trouble
we should first seek to realize God's presence with us.
Only let's enjoy His smile, and we can bear our daily cross
with a willing heart for His dear sake."
—Charles Spurgeon

I started gently weaning the kids off the idea that their dad was going to recover. We had had moments of doubt, to be sure, but we always talked as if Dad would get better and come home eventually. Becky and I have always mirrored each other emotionally throughout this, so when I brought it up, she merely said, "Mom, I know."

Rachel and Daniel fought the idea for a while. We'd been praying that God might wake or take Dad, so when I mentioned that I thought God had turned down our request, they got kind of angry. Their eyes welled up with tears and they asked me, "Don't you think God can heal Daddy anymore?"

I said, "No, I still think He can; I just don't think He's going to."

23

"For Better For Worse"

July 24, 2004

> *Faith means believing in advance*
> *what will only make sense in reverse.*
> —*Where is God When it Hurts*, by Philip Yancey

Dear Family and Friends,

What a confusing, challenging, hard, exhausting year. For some reason, I keep picturing a snow globe in my mind. You know, one of those pretty things you see on the store shelves at Christmas time? Daniel and I can't resist grabbing them and giving them a great big shake. Instant blizzard!

Life for our family the past two years has seemed like that snow globe. (Can anyone relate?) Finally, the storm has passed and even though the snow is gradually settling, we are still a little stunned and dizzy from the whole experience. I think, too, that our globe was not only shaken, but hurled against a wall, because while the glass is still intact, some of the pieces inside are broken or missing. It just isn't the same. One thing remains unchanged, however, and that is the character of God. Three hundred and sixty five days ago, He was good. He is still good today. "I the Lord do not change." Malachi 3:6

> *Our circumstances are not*
> *an accurate reflection*
> *of God's goodness.*
> *Whether life is good or bad, God's goodness,*
> *rooted in His character, is the same.*
> —Helen Grace Lescheid

Jimmy Carter once quoted his high school teacher Miss Julia Coleman in his 1977 inaugural address, saying, "We must adjust to changing times and still hold to *unchanging principles." It may be out of context, but I was thinking that this idea could be applied to our relationships with God.*

When life spins out of our control, we frail human beings need an anchor to cast into the angry waves, a fortress to run into, a solid rock to stand on. I am so grateful that God is all those things and much, much more. I praise Him for never changing, for never failing, for His steadfast love.

Today marks the anniversary of Tim's accident. We were easily distracted from that fact all day as life kept us extremely busy. There probably wouldn't have been a whole lot of emotion even if we weren't distracted, though. Our friend, Don, was visiting from Japan last week and he commented, "Wow, you all seem so strong." I told him I wasn't sure if it was strength or numbness that allowed us to talk about Tim without falling apart. Probably a little of both. It is comforting to know that God understands even this about us. I can pray to Him with complete honesty saying, "I love you, Lord, but I just can't muster up any feeling to go with those words anymore. I'm too tired and too emotionally spent. All I have left to offer you is my will—today I choose to believe you and obey you."

When circumstances seem impossible, when all signs of grace in you seem at their lowest ebb, when temptation is fiercest, when love and joy and hope seem well-nigh extinguished in your heart, then rest, without feeling and without emotion,
in the Father's faithfulness.
—D. Tryon

There has been no change in Tim's condition. He has not had a major infection for three months now. Today, he felt slightly warm, and I wondered if his UTI might be returning. I suspect that they cannot completely rid him of the bad bugs that he has had in the past. I think they're just beaten back into submission for a while with antibiotics because every few months the infection seems to return with a vengeance.

It has been a tough year, and Tim has definitely had the worst of it, but wherever my husband is, I know that he continues to believe that His Savior has not abandoned him. I hurt for Tim seeing him in this condition, but I firmly believe that God will deliver him when the time is right. I got up one morning this week and thanked God for helping me to hang on another day, and then I mused, "Will it always be like this? Will Tim be like this for years and years? I can't say that I can't take it another day because I have taken it day after day for an entire year. I realize now that with Your help, I could do this until You come again.

I just don't want Tim to have to endure a life like this day after day. "How long, O Lord, how long?(Psalm 6:3)" A few hours later Rae and I were sitting together at Starbucks doing our weekly Bible study. It just so happened that the lesson began talk-

ing about Job's trial. One comment leapt off the page at me. Paraphrased, it said, "Then just as suddenly as Job's trial began, it came to an end."

I thought back to the day Tim was injured—it was so unexpected, so out of the blue. Tim had absolutely no hint that life as he knew it was over. Tim's trial will end someday just as suddenly as it began. In the meantime, may we all faithfully endure. Thanks so much for being the presence of God to my family these past two years. We wouldn't have made it without you. We love you.

God bless you,
Carole and the kids

August 10, 2004

> *Dear Family and Friends,*
> *A very interesting thing happened yesterday. Got a call from the Bush/Cheney campaign. A few months ago, Daniel came to me and asked me if I thought that President Bush would read a letter from him if Dan sent one. I said he might and asked him what he wanted to write to the President. He said, "You and Daddy told us that President Bush is a real godly man, and I wanted to tell him about Daddy and ask him to pray for him."*
> *So, we sat down and Daniel dictated a brief letter to the president. We popped it in the mail and over the next few weeks, Dan would occasionally ask if I thought the president got his letter. I told him I thought so. About ten days ago, I received a call from the White House Correspondence Office. The gentleman who called said the White House had received Dan's letter, and that they were very touched by it. He inquired about Tim's condition. Then, he said the President would personally read Dan's letter. We were all pretty excited about that. It meant so much to Daniel.*
> *Yesterday, when the Bush/Cheney campaign called, they said President Bush would be in Phoenix for a rally on Wednesday and that the President had really been touched by Daniel's letter about Tim. He said his letter had become well known throughout the entire campaign. Wow. Then came the real wow. The deputy campaign director of the Southwest Region said President Bush would like to meet Daniel on Wednesday in person. I was stunned.*
> *Unfortunately, Daniel is in Michigan right now and wouldn't be home by Wednesday! He was in the middle of a much anticipated two-week camping/fishing/ water skiing/motor cycle riding "guys only" summer vacation at his Uncle John's house. When I told Daniel about it, he was very excited, and we talked about him coming home a little early, but (long story short) it just wouldn't work out. So, he dic-*

tated another letter to the President, and we hope to get it into his hands somehow. The girls and I were offered VIP tickets to the rally, so we will be going to cheer on our very excellent President tomorrow evening.

Life continually amazes me. Tim would be flabbergasted by all of this, but delighted to know that his kids had turned into staunch little Republicans like Mom and Dad. When I told the girls that the President wanted to meet Daniel, they screamed (like the teeny boppers that they are) as if Orlando Bloom had walked into the room. Shows you how politics rate around this house. I will keep you posted on Tim's condition.

Love,
Carole

October 15, 2004

Dear Family and Friends,

"I don't want to sound cold, and I know you are a spiritual family but at what point in time do you decide to put the pillow over his face and straddle him? You are in my prayers. His quality of life is gone! God has left it up to you!"
Welcome to my nervous breakdown.

I hadn't checked the Web site in a while, and this is what I found in the guest book upon my return. I am not acquainted with the person who wrote this message, but more importantly, they are not acquainted with Tim or me because if they were, they would know the answer to their question: BECAUSE WE ARE NOT GOD. I don't even play Him on TV. If the job were open, I wouldn't apply because I'd make a lousy God. I have some talents, but creating and running the universe is not among them, and I do not recall seeing "Giver and Taker of life" in my current job description anywhere.

Please don't think I am offended by this person's comments. I am not. But I am thankful for an opportunity to respond and be completely honest with you about what has been transpiring lately.

Two months ago, I basically abandoned this Web site because I was struggling with all of the issues that have resulted from Tim being left in a vegetative state. It has been over a year since Tim's accident, and I have begun to face decisions that I would not wish on my worst enemy. I am in the middle of a great big mess, y'all, with some folks on the one hand urging me to be fair to Tim, to be his advocate and to turn off his tube, and others saying, "How could you even think of such a thing?"

The kids and I are well aware that Tim is not experiencing life. That's one of the reasons I don't post updates anymore because there is absolutely nothing to tell you about Tim. He does not participate in life in any way anymore. He isn't brain dead, just very, very severely, permanently brain damaged. All that he has been left with are some very basic body functions and reflexive, non-purposeful movements, and very infrequently, the ability to follow some commands without knowing it.

He is suffering—and frankly, we are, too. There are days when I feel that I will lose my sanity watching him languish in that bed. We pray and plead with God daily to take Tim home, to make him whole and well again, to end his suffering. We ask God to allow the deep wound that the kids and I have sustained to finally begin to heal. As it is right now, the pain never goes away. It is constantly there. Our lives are in a state of limbo and we have to deal with the anguish of seeing Tim suffer on a daily basis, as well as deal with myriad guilt feelings. Guilt over trying to go on with our lives while Tim is denied any kind of life, guilt over medical decisions I have made in the past and present, and the guilt over the relief that we would feel if this were all to end tomorrow.

Tim would not want to linger on like this. I know that for a fact and so does everyone who really knows Tim intimately. He verbally told me what his wishes were if he was ever found in this type of situation. He wouldn't want this to continue. He would much rather be home with the Lord. Tim was homesick for heaven when he was happy and healthy. How much more so now.

Having said all of this, I have prayerfully concluded that regardless of Tim's wishes or our desires, neither of us is God. I'm sure Tim's had enough of all of this, and believe me, I have, too. But, it's just not our call. I see no Scriptures that advocate euthanasia, but I do see a ton of examples of impatient human beings saying to themselves, "Oh, no ... looks like God's asleep at the switch. I'd better start fiddling." And the results have always been disastrous. I have absolute confidence that God hasn't forgotten Tim, that He still knows what He is doing, and that He will take Tim home when the time is exactly right.

God doesn't need my assistance, or the assistance of the doctors, hospice, or anyone else for that matter. God has not left this up to me. My life has never been more out of my control. Tim, the kids, and I may not like it, but we are going to sit in our "prison cell," just like Joseph, until God personally delivers us.

It's a sad way to live, and I have often wished I hadn't survived my battle with cancer. Then I wouldn't have had to see what I have seen, I wouldn't have had to face any of this. I'd love a quicker way out, and, oh, how I have prayed for someone to come along and take my place and do this better if they could. I've raged and raged at God, but each time the tears and the tantrums subside, I always come back to the same basic, unchanging truths. I may say them less enthusiastically because I am so very tired, but they are true nonetheless.

Many have asked how Tim is doing these days. He is well cared for at Sunbridge and is not sick at present. The only thing we have noticed is that his "sleep cycle" seems to be getting longer and he has periods of apnea. I am sorry that the kids and I don't talk about Tim more. It is difficult to talk about him to anyone but each other.

I have been trying really hard to listen to God so I haven't had much to say to you of late. But, I felt compelled to write after reading this comment in the guest book. People have mostly responded to our situation with kindness and compassion, but every once in a while, I hear two things that do not sit well with me. The first is any type of comment that somehow God has lost control of our situation and the second is the notion that this could never happen to you. These two ideas come at me in various forms, but this is what they all boil down to. I can't say for sure what God is trying to accomplish through our situation, but I am certain He is not looking for these two responses.

God is sovereign and no matter how loudly we shout, "You're not the boss of me!" the fact is He is the Boss. He can do whatever He likes with our lives (and He does) whether we enjoy it, understand it, and cooperate with Him or not. Please remember to temper this knowledge of God's ways with the incredible knowledge of the love of God demonstrated so beautifully on the cross. His ways are unfathomable, but so is His love. He does what He does with our ultimate good uppermost in His mind. He's not some malevolent bully who likes watching us squirm like ants under a magnifying glass on a bright, sunny day.

Secondly, while I hope that you never find yourself in a similar situation to ours, please realize that this could happen to you—or maybe something worse could happen. (Hey, there's a cheerful thought.) I'm not trying to be the scary preacher in Pollyanna who keeps shouting, "DEATH COMES UNEXPECTEDLY!" but my question to you is—are you prepared if this were your last day on earth? I'm not just talking about having your earthly affairs in order and your will drawn up. I'm talking about your standing with God.

Tim was a wonderful person, and I know that if he were to die today, he would spend eternity with God—not because he was a wonderful person, but because he has a personal relationship with Jesus Christ. There was a point in his life when he realized that heaven, eternal life, was a gift to be received and not something to be earned or deserved.

"For by grace you have been saved through faith and that not of yourselves, it is the gift of God, not as a result of works so that no one should boast."
(Ephesians 2:8–9)

This makes sense when you really think about it. None of us could ever earn our way to heaven because we have all sinned and sin deserves to be punished. We might try to "pay for" our sins ourselves by doing lots of good deeds or by going to church a lot, but that does nothing to get rid of them. The Bible says that the wages of sin is death. Separation from God for all eternity—that's what we deserve, not heaven.

Tim used to say that he loved me so much that if he could die to pay for my sins he would. Except there was a problem ... he would be too busy dying for his own sins. We can't save ourselves or anyone else for that matter because we have all missed the mark and fallen short of God's standard—which is perfect holiness—that's the bad news.

The good news is that heaven is a free gift—that doesn't mean it wasn't costly. It just means that it didn't cost us anything. It cost God everything, however. Seeing that we could not save ourselves, God came in the flesh to do what we could never do. He lived a perfectly sinless life and then He willingly paid the price of heaven for all of us by suffering and dying on the cross.

Acts 16 says, "Believe on the Lord Jesus Christ and you will be saved." Years ago, Tim placed his faith completely in what Christ alone had done for him on the cross. Tim had absolute assurance that one day he would be with the Lord, and I hope and pray that you have that assurance, as well. I pray that you would grow to realize just how much the great God of the universe loves you, remember that none of your hurts will be wasted by Him, and trust Him implicitly.

That's what I'm trying to do, but I fail so miserably at times. My mind has turned into a battlefield of warring thoughts. I try to be steadfast and believe, but sometimes I'm too tired to fight and too spent to care. I chuck my sword, sit down in the dirt, and cry. This path that we're walking on right now is exhausting, steep, dark, lonely, and feels like it's never going to end. I've asked God so many times this past month to give me just a sliver of an idea of what is going on. Enlighten me, please!

It would be so much easier to get up and face another day if I only had a clue as to what was happening or how long we had to keep this up. But, God has asked me to simply trust Him. It's not a blind trust because I can look back on thousands of years of recorded history in the Bible, and not once did God fail to keep His word. I have twenty plus years of personal experience with Him, too, and He has never let me down.

Sometimes on a really bad day, I feel like He's let me down this time, but I have to remind myself it's not over yet. It ain't over 'til the trumpet sounds.

Someday, hopefully soon, all of our questions will be answered. In the meantime we need to always remember that God will never, ever abandon us or turn a deaf ear to our cries. We are never forsaken, though we feel like it at times. God perfectly understands and sympathizes with our plight because He's "been there, done that," too. Remember the cross?

    As always, we appreciate your prayers. And to the person who wrote me that note—thanks for your opinion. The next time I want your opinion, though, I'll just beat it out of you. Just kidding!

Love,

Carole

24

"In Joy and In Sorrow"

One day, I stopped in to see Tim's attending physician. I had some paperwork for him to sign, and after he looked it over, he sat down across from me and asked how our family was holding up. We talked a while about how Tim was faring. I pointed out that Tim had been in a coma for over a year, and I wondered if doctors would treat him differently from here on out.

At twelve months, a vegetative state is considered permanent, and there probably wasn't a reputable doctor in the universe who would tell me that Tim had a chance of recovering now.

Tim's doctor said, "Absolutely." Then he asked me if Tim had ever expressed his wishes about the end of his life.

I couldn't believe it. This was the first time in over twelve months that somebody asked me what Tim wanted. I had been asked what I wanted to do and been told what Tim needed to have done to him, but no one had ever asked me about Tim's wishes. I told him what Tim had expressed, and I said I had often questioned some of the decisions that I had made regarding his care. But, I said, too, if I had to do things over again, I would most likely do the exact same thing. I believed what the doctors had told me from the start, but felt that I needed to give Tim a chance, to explore every possibility. I needed to give God time to do a miracle. I probably would have always wondered, "What if?" had we not aggressively saved Tim's life.

He said, "Carole, it's time to do what Tim wants. You're his wife, his guardian, his representative—you need to think of what he would want and not what you want. You're Tim's voice now."

He encouraged me to think through things and make those hard decisions now, while Tim was doing well. He urged me not to wait until a crisis came because it would be difficult to think clearly.

I asked him what kind of decisions he was talking about. He said, "Well, do you want Tim treated anymore? We could stop all of his medications. We could turn off his feeding tube and just let him go."

I said when I next saw Tim in heaven, I was probably going to get a good shaking before I even got a hug. I figured Tim would say, "Carole, what were you thinking? I told you NO TUBES! I could have been home months ago!"

But, the tube was in and euthanasia was out. As for Tim's current meds—I didn't want anything changed. He was still to get blood thinners, heart meds, vitamins, stomach meds—whatever he was getting now should continue. As for further treatment ... I didn't really know. I said I wanted to pray about things and get some counsel from my pastor.

I called Tami and Pastor Steve and asked if we could meet, and then I prayed that God would confirm what I felt was the right thing to do. We met at Chili's for lunch and after chatting for a while, Steve, who likes to get to the point, said, "So, what's up?"

I started weeping as I told them about my conversation with the doctor. I said I wasn't entirely sure what to do. I said I wondered if I'd been doing the right thing regarding Tim. I wondered if I was getting in God's way, kind of like the guy I once heard about in a joke about a flood ... *A flood approaches a town and all the inhabitants are told to evacuate. One very spiritual man prays that God would rescue him. A truck drives up to his house and the people inside yell, "Get in!" but the man says, "No thanks. God's going to save me."*

As the floodwaters begin to rise, the man is forced upstairs. A motor boat sails up to his bedroom window and the people in the boat yell, "Get in!" The man again says, "No, thanks. God's going to save me."

Finally, the waters are so high that the man is forced to climb onto the roof of his house. A helicopter hovers overhead and the people inside throw down a rope and yell, "Grab on!" Once again, the man says, "No, thanks. God's going to save me."

Finally the man drowns. He ends up in heaven, and he approaches the Lord and says, "What gives? I prayed and believed that you were going to save me. Why didn't You?" God replied, "Son, you're not the brightest one I ever created, are you? I sent you a truck, and a boat, and a helicopter!!"

My point was, I had been praying all along for God's deliverance, and Tim had been so close to the threshold of heaven several times. Had I done too much in my effort to hang onto him? Had I let the doctors go too far? Had God tried to take Tim home and I had prevented Him?

They both encouraged me so much and said they felt that the decisions I had made about Tim thus far had been great and that God had been guiding me.

Steve said he believed God would continue to guide me as things came up and assured me that no one was capable of thwarting God. If God wanted Tim, God would take Tim. He said he knew Tim would much rather be home with the Lord, but he said, too, that he didn't think it was right to withhold nutrition and water. He said as far as further treatment went to maybe take it day by day. If something simple came up and an antibiotic could knock it out easily, then go ahead. But, if something really life threatening came up—well, he felt that God would let me know what to do and when to do it. He reminded me that the only thing we knew for sure about Tim was that he felt pain. I knew what he was getting at with that comment.

After meeting with them, I was relieved and felt like I had gotten the confirmation I had prayed for. Later in the week, I called Tim's doctor and said to continue Tim's current treatment and current nutrition. I told him I decided that we had had enough of hospitals and emergency rooms, though. Those places couldn't cure him, and no matter what you said to them, they often went overboard in a case like Tim's and caused him terrific pain. Tim would stay at Sunbridge for all treatments, and we would see how it went.

Later on, I called Kay, Tim's mom. All along, Kay had been 100 percent supportive of every decision I had made, and she continued being supportive. She said she felt that I was doing the right thing. I was so grateful to Tim's extended family for being such an encouragement to me; especially as I saw the events surrounding the Schiavo case unfold in Florida.

Right after this, Tim got sick. I was terrified and thought if I didn't let them pop Tim in an ambulance and rush him to the hospital that he would die and it would be all my fault. He was pretty ill for a couple of days, and I was beginning to second guess myself, and then suddenly, he turned the corner and began to recover.

Maybe I'm reading into things here, but I believed God was trying to tell me something. I think He wanted me to know that no matter what I did, or what anyone did, that He was in charge. Tim was His responsibility and I could take the shingle that said, "Head Hog of the Trough" down from my door. Tim wouldn't leave this earth one second sooner or later than God had ordained.

As I was sitting with Tim one day, one of the nurses came up to me and asked me if I would like to meet with the folks from hospice. I said, "What for? Tim's not dying!"

She explained that usually when someone went on hospice that they only had six months or less to live, but in cases like Tim's, people could be on hospice care for years. She further explained that Tim would get even better care and extra services being on hospice. Even more importantly, she said the kids and I would receive support, and if Tim took a sudden turn for the worse, things would be in place to make that time as painless as possible for all of us.

I agreed to meet with them and the next day, I had a brief meeting with one of the hospice workers. Tim was approved and his care really did get even better. He started getting extra showers and extra visits from hospice workers. They are the neatest folks in the world. Hearts of gold, and they became really attached to Tim. I really loved these folks. They called the kids and me and constantly offered help. Their chaplain would stop by to pray with us, and they were so kind to my husband.

Everyone at Sunbridge loved Tim, though. He was one of the younger residents in the nursing home and very good looking. Once a speech therapist that had worked with Tim at Palm Valley stopped by to say hi. She commented that it didn't matter when she stopped in to see Tim, he always looked so nice.

Another social worker at Sunbridge once said she marveled that Tim never had bed head. "All the residents who are bedridden have messy hair," she said, "but Tim's is always beautiful." The staff and I were forever brushing Tim's hair and I always raced to Sunbridge in the mornings so that I could be the one to shave Tim. Poor Tim never got out of a shave, not even on the weekends. When he was well, he used to take Saturdays off from shaving, but since I had become his personal barber, he never got a break.

One of Tim's roommates at Sunbridge even became like a bodyguard for Tim. Randy was a really big guy and came off quite gruff and grumpy. He didn't get along with some of the nurses, and I was a little intimidated by him. He rarely spoke to me.

Tim fell ill again, and I had been spending the nights there. At one point, someone came in to give Tim a shower, and I had sent them away. I thanked them, but said Tim wasn't feeling well and I didn't want anyone to bother him. After a day or two, Tim finally felt better, and I'd gone home. Evidently, someone had come by to shower Tim, and Randy told them to go away! He said, "Carole doesn't want anybody messing with Tim when he's not feeling well. Scram!"

My mom had dropped by, and Randy proudly told her how he'd chased off the CNAs! After that, we became good friends and every time I got to Tim's room, Randy would give me a report. He'd tell me who stopped by, mention if he thought Tim was coughing more than usual—things like that. I don't know why he warmed up to us so much.

Three months after Tim was placed on hospice care, I was asked to a meeting. Tim's hospice team was all there and the social worker from Sunbridge. They asked me what my plans for Tim were. I was confused and said I didn't have any plans. As the meeting progressed, I realized that some of the folks at the meeting (not all of them) were urging me to turn off Tim's feeding tube. They said it was the right thing to do, and the way that they put it made me feel so guilty.

I'm sure the hospice workers had no idea of the tremendous impact of their words. Words can leave our mouths in a very straightforward manner, but that doesn't mean they travel in a straight line to our recipients' ear. Words can get intercepted by the emotions and circumstances of our listener, magnifying and coloring their meaning.

For example, in the months after Tim's injury, doctors had approached me and said, "Your husband really NEEDS this (tube, test, shunt, drain, catheter, antibiotic, respirator, or whatever). If I had been told by a doctor that standing on my head and spitting nickels would benefit Tim, I would have at least tried it because what I was really hearing from the docs was, "You are responsible for this man that you love, and if you don't do this thing, he will suffer more and it will be all your fault." That's not what they *said,* but that's what I *heard.*

I was devastated to be told that Tim's tube should come out. In effect I felt I was being told that I'd made a huge mistake allowing the feeding tube in the first place. I was told that Tim was suffering, but what I heard was Tim's suffering was all my fault. The tube had always been a sensitive area for me because the doctors said Tim needed it but I knew that Tim wouldn't have wanted it.

Part of me wished that I could comply with them for Tim, but I just couldn't. What was done was done. Also, our decisions are based on our convictions. Euthanizing or mercy killing, if you prefer a less potent expression, was a moral no-no to me. If I was already feeling bad about putting in the feeding tube, imagine the struggle to live with myself if I allowed them to remove it and euthanize Tim!

Then, someone suggested decreasing the amount of nutrition Tim was receiving. I was really confused by this time, and Eleanor, the hospice nurse, finally suggested that I should discuss this with Tim's doctor. (Tim had a new attending physician). I remember that I was asked what I would do if Tim's body started failing because force feeding someone at that point can actually cause them more harm than good. I said I didn't know that, and that I guessed I would worry about that when it happened. I walked out of that meeting confused and feeling like such a rotten person. Someone at the meeting meant well, I'm sure, but at one point they'd said to me, "Carole, what would Jesus do? Jesus wouldn't let Tim continue to suffer like this and you shouldn't either. Tim's told you what he wanted. You are obligated to carry out his wishes." I'd almost been guilted into telling them to yank out Tim's tube.

Again, I prayed for confirmation for the decisions I had made. I prayed for God to remove this decision from my hands. Fallible human beings have no business meddling with these things! We're just not qualified to decide who deserves to live and who deserves to die.

I met a few days later with Tim's new doctor, and he said he just wanted me to know he would never authorize turning down or turning off Tim's tube. "He was a Christian," he said, "and didn't believe that it was moral to do that." Tim's doctor and I were in total agreement about Tim's care.

Amazingly, there were no hard feelings between the hospice team and me. They respected my decisions and continued to be a source of help and comfort to my family. In fact, a few weeks later, a nurse from the hospice organization's central office called me at home. She asked me if I would be willing to be interviewed for a video that they were making that would be used by hospice as a training tool.

As she explained further, she said she wanted to videotape Tim and me together at his room. I balked at that idea. I think I felt embarrassed for Tim. I didn't think he would want thousands of people watching him in this condition. She promised that it would be very dignified and very respectful. She went on to say that their entire organization had heard of our family and that we were highly respected for the stands we had taken on Tim's care and for our faith in God.

I agreed to do it. It wasn't that I wanted to make a video, but I felt that I should and that this was another opportunity placed in front of me by God. There had been so many things like this that had happened over the past several months, and each time I remember thinking, "This is part of the reason why this happened to our family."

I'd been asked to speak at a ladies Bible conference and also a Bible study. I had turned them down with a, "Maybe some day when I'm not still in the middle of it." I'd even begun writing a book about our experience. I was asked to do things that were so far out of my comfort zone, so far removed from what I thought I was capable of, and it was a little scary. But I knew that in trusting God to accomplish these "good works that He prepared beforehand," for me to walk in that He would be glorified because it would be obvious to everyone who really knew me that it was God's work and not mine. My job was to be obedient as these things came up.

Tim was just getting over another infection, so I had been staying at his room for several nights, and I was very tired. Ann, the RN who interviewed me, was a very kind person. She brought along another gal who videotaped the interview. At first, I just sat with Tim in his room and did what I normally did. I held his hand and talked to him. The ladies were silent for so long, and I was getting sleepy, so I turned around to ask them how much longer they were going to film us and found Ann silently crying.

After that, we went into one of the rec rooms, and I was gently interviewed for about 45 minutes. Wow, that was hard. They asked me all about Tim's accident and the entire experience that our family had been through, and as I recollected the past months and attempted to verbalize it, I kept breaking down. I could relate facts about Tim, but the moment somebody asked the kids and I how we *felt* about what was going on, the tears, which were always just below the surface, would break through in torrents.

I think that's one of the reasons I wrote so much on the Web site. It was so much easier to sit alone at a keyboard and write about how you felt. If you cried while you were doing it, no one would know. I know that people understood the tears and the emotions, but nobody likes to grieve in public.

After the interview, Ann hugged me and thanked me for sharing our story. Our case was unique, she said, in that our family was fairly young compared to a lot of the families that they normally worked with. She said, too, that family members weren't always able to articulate what they were going through and that hearing firsthand what we'd gone through, learning about our struggles along the way and the problems we had encountered would be so helpful in training hospice workers. Before they can meet needs, they have to be able to recognize them.

25

"In God's Presence"

November 6, 2004

Dear Family and Friends,

 Watching the recent presidential election reminded me of something … Daniel's letter. Daniel, if you recall, was invited to meet President Bush a couple of months ago after writing a letter about his dad. Unfortunately, Dan was out of state at the time and was unable to meet with the President. A few days later, Daniel received a manila envelope in the mail from the White House. We thought, perhaps, that the President's office had sent Dan a photo of George Bush, but it turned out to be a personal letter from the President.

 I got such a kick out of Daniel on Election Day. On November 2, Daniel was glued to the television set from 6 p.m. until midnight watching the results pour in. I watched with him for quite a while and each time President Bush extended his lead, Daniel would jump up from his chair and holler, "YES!" and high five me. After a while, I left the room to work on the computer. All evening long, Daniel would occasionally tear into the room and yell, "Mom, Mom, President Bush just got 20 more points! Now the score is 204 to 144!" Later, he ran in and grabbed some paper and a pen so he could "keep score." Frustrated that the election ticker results were going by too quickly for him to write anything down, Dan then got out our digital camera so that he could take his own screen captures to keep track of what was going on.

 The kids and I stayed up until midnight watching the election. Daniel finally started falling asleep in his dad's chair, so I sent him off to bed. He was hugely disappointed that a winner hadn't been declared yet, but was confident that his man would win. Thank God, President Bush won! I don't know what Daniel would have done if "W" hadn't prevailed.

 Love,
 Carole

January 1, 2005

Dear Family and Friends,

    I am probably in a minority when I say this, but I LOVE yearly letters. Doesn't matter if I get them at Christmas, New Year's, or on the Fourth of July, I just love them. (Incidentally, if you sent us a photo this year, you're on my fridge!)

    I kicked around the idea of composing a yearly letter to send out at Christmas time, but quickly gave up on the notion due to the "series of unfortunate events" that our family has recently experienced. Annual letters should be cheerful and full of mostly pleasant anecdotes, don't you think? I have found that once folks start hearing our tale, their eyes begin to widen, and they unconsciously start backing away from me. They don't want to stand next to me in the grocery line, let alone hear from me in a letter. Can't say I blame them, really. Besides, penning our yearly letter was always Tim's forte. He injected his quirky brand of humor into each one, making them fun to receive.

    For the family and folks that are faithfully checking our site, however, I submit our year-end report:

    Daniel: Twelve years old. Sixth grade. Handsome. Ninety pounds of solid muscle. Wears the biggest shoes in the household. Five feet-one inch and growing nightly, I might add. Never ceases to mention that he's gaining on his five foot-three inch Mom, who weighs in at … well, never you mind. According to Tim's grandma, during the seventh grade, Tim grew about eight inches. She claims he would have been 7 feet tall if so much of him hadn't turned under (Tim's a size 13). I predict that Dan will do the exact same thing. Looks like his daddy, and it is Mom's prayer that he will emulate his father's outstanding character as well. (So far, so good.)

    Still home schooled, he is active in the Jr. High Youth Group at church, as well as AWANA clubs. He is currently a green belt with a white stripe in the martial art of Tang Soo Do. Says he likes breaking boards the best. Next belt will be brown. Loves video games, learning the electric guitar, and the Jr. NRA rifle class that he attends every week. (Are we the stereotypical, geeky homeschoolers, or what?)

    Dan and Mom appreciate the men who have come alongside him this year to stand in his father's place—mentoring, teaching, wrestling, teasing, and generally giving him a break from us girly girls.

    Rachel: Sweet sixteen and never been kissed—and I wouldn't recommend trying to steal one from her either. As lethal as she is beautiful, Rae is now an award-winning red belt in Tang Soo Do, after claiming a 1st place and two 2nd places at her first-ever regional championship in October. A home-schooled junior, she is creative, passionate, articulate, artistic, loves sketching, woodworking, music, and books. A tomboy to the core, family and friends, with cameras in tow, stalked her like the paparazzi after she donned a skirt for her performance in the church dinner theater.

She is eccentric in taste (but aren't most artists?) and likes anything from combat boots to weapons to fedoras. Recently started working part-time alongside her sister at the local theater. It has been the best thing for her, keeping her busy and giving her an opportunity to be normal again as no one at the theater knows about her dad. It gets tough on the kids to constantly be defined by their family's trials and tragedies.

Actively helps out with the AWANA program and sings in the church choir. Participated in the inspirational Christmas dinner theater put on by our church that I am sure touched many, many lives. Learning the bass guitar. Slender and looks like daddy. Probably the offspring that reminds me of Tim the most, especially in the humor department.

Becky: Affectionately known as "The Princess" around here, she is beautiful, smart, chic, and a snappy dresser. Could pass for 25 because she is so composed and mature. Vocally talented like her sister, she sings with the church choir and often performs special music. She, too, participated in the dinner theater—absolutely loved the costumes, which were from the 1940s era. Becky would be thrilled if those styles, or even ball gowns, came back into fashion.

Computer savvy but definitely not a nerd. Has learned the fine art of stiff-arming the fellahs like a linebacker to fend off those requests for a date. "No thank you. I'm not planning to date until I am older and ready for a relationship." (Praise the Lord, and Mom breathes a huge sigh of relief) On her eighteenth birthday, she received a call from Arizona State University congratulating her on her admission to the university next fall.

Final year of home schooling. Plans to participate in the Arizona Families for Home Education Graduation ceremony this coming May. Active in the AWANA ministry with the littlest ones, the Cubbies, she also works part-time at the local theater where she was recently promoted to team leader. Discerning like her father, but a definite "Mini Me" in appearance, right down to the red hair, freckles, and manner of walking. She is my right-hand gal.

Carole: Busy, busy … did I mention busy? Also a snappy dresser (sometimes) because Becky tells her what to wear. Can't survive without her Palm Pilot. Neat freak. Loves to cook. Also loves to eat, which is one reason why she loves to run. AWANA Commander at church—loves being with the kiddos. Soon to be working part-time at church as the Children's Ministry Director—pray for her! Enjoys home schooling—can't believe she's old enough to have a daughter going off to college.

Attempting to learn the guitar with Becky. Probably doesn't smile or laugh as much as she used to, but just can't help herself when someone comments that she has it all together. Extremely appreciative of her family and dear friends. Knows that she couldn't have survived these past months without them. At peace with God after exchanging her nervous breakdown for a breakthrough in November (more on that later). Has found a new stress reliever—joined the Annie Oakley Sure Shots with her daughters. Once a week, they spend the evening shooting the dickens out of paper plates at the shooting range as the teenagers shout, "We WILL maintain our virginity until we're married—and we'll use force if necessary!" Laughs all the way home.

Plans for the New Year include trying to avoid catastrophe (no guarantees there) and reading through the Bible as a family. (Pastor has challenged our entire church to read through the Bible this year) Considering a family mission trip this summer.

As for Tim ... no change. He has good days where his health is OK and bad days where he is sick or uncomfortable. His last major illness was around Thanksgiving. Those times where he is fighting an infection are the toughest for me. As I sit there and watch him struggle, I feel myself getting more and more depressed and angry at God. Not that I blame Him for Tim's accident, but I guess I have been holding Tim's present condition against Him. After all, He could mercifully bring this trial to an end and for whatever reason, He doesn't.

As I sat with Tim through the long hours, our dear friend Jim H. stopped by. We sat holding Tim's hands and talked. He told me of two conversations that he had had with Tim. One conversation occurred when Jim's wife, Mimi, was diagnosed with breast cancer (she is a survivor), and the other conversation occurred when I was fighting breast cancer years later. Jim and Tim were real close friends and both of them had the same thing to say when their families were facing these trials. "If this is necessary, Lord, then bring it on." That's Tim all right.

Then Jim said he couldn't wait for Tim to be able to tell us what he was experiencing while in a coma. Jim said he guessed that Tim was having a very special, incredible time with the Lord. His comment stopped me in my tracks, and I was immediately reminded of those months where I was battling cancer. It had been a very difficult time physically, but an incredible, joyful time spiritually. I experienced God's presence in a way that was so wonderful that, at times, I felt euphoric. It is difficult to put into words, really, but God knows when His children are hurting. He cares and He comes near. I know I am not the only one to say this. Mimi will tell you the exact same thing. I've read countless stories of people facing all sorts of trials and suffering, and they all say the same thing, too.

As I remembered this, I turned and looked at Tim. For the first time since his accident, I was able to look past Tim's broken body and picture him enjoying sweet com-

munion with God, and I thought, "No wonder you didn't come back to us, you rascal. I don't blame you one bit." I can't stand the thought of Tim lying in that bed suffering every single day for who knows how much longer. But, I can stand the thought of Tim being nearer to God than he's ever been.

I don't think that Tim is aware of what he is going through physically. He doesn't know me, or the kids, or even who he is anymore. I do think that he is aware in God's presence, though, of what is happening. I think he has been shown the Plan.

I picture the Lord putting His arm around Tim and saying, "Son, I want to show you something."

He stretches out His arm, and Tim is able to see everything from start to finish.

Tim exclaims, "Lord, You're brilliant! It's such an excellent plan. Every single little detail is worked out perfectly. It is truly amazing."

Then the Lord says, "Yes, but you realize that this plan includes a great deal of suffering on your part?"

Tim immediately says, "That's OK with me. Bring it on. I can see how it all fits together, how it all works out. Go for it."

Then the Lord says, "Alright, but you also realize that your family will endure a great deal of pain as well?"

At this Tim would balk a little. He'd say sadly, "Lord, must You allow them to hurt so? Isn't there some other way?"

The Lord would reply, "It is necessary."

Then Tim would finally say, "All right. Bring it on. You'll see I didn't raise a single wimp in my household."

That's how I picture Tim right now. Hey, whatever gets you through the day, right?

This morning, I received a call from our realtor. The company that handled the purchase of our home sure knows customer service. They mail out coupons for pies around the holidays, host free movie nights at the local theater, and make frequent contacts with former clients. When the realtor called, he asked me if I realized that we'd been in our house for ten months already. I hadn't. We talked for a few minutes about the real estate market in my neighborhood (it's very, very good, but I am NOT moving again, Lord willing) and then he asked if he could ask me a personal question. I said sure.

He had been wondering for months the secret to our family's peace. He said he marveled at our ability to stay so upbeat in the midst of our situation and had even told others about us.

I said it was all a matter of perspective. Our family's perspective was a direct result of our relationship with God. I explained further as we talked for a little while longer. After we hung up, the kids were curious to know who I was talking to. We had been reading together before the phone rang, so they had been sitting there listening to my end of the conversation. I looked at them and said, "God is still at work in our situation. We probably don't see it because we are still in the middle of it all, but we're living supernaturally. We're living and experiencing God's power, presence, and grace in such a way that people who meet us want to know our 'secret.' That's pretty cool, huh?"

Honestly, it doesn't feel very cool right now. I am sure there are many, many of you who feel the same way. Someday, we will be able to see the whole Plan, too. I am sure at that time we will all feel that this has been worth it, that it has been an awesome thing to take part in. Not right now, though. For right now, we're just thankful to get through each day.

Maranatha,
Carole, Becky, Rachel, and Daniel

Tim's mom and her husband, Jim, came for another visit. Seeing for themselves that Tim had made no progress at all since they had last seen him was a huge disappointment. Jim managed an office full of doctors, and he told me that after reading the update mentioning the change in Tim's breathing, he had gone to one of the doctors he worked with and asked them what it meant. He said, "It is not a good sign. It means that Tim is losing even more brain function." Jim also said seeing Tim again made them realize he was gone and that all we really had here was Tim's body.

And that, my friends, is how I would describe a vegetative state to you. It's like being a living corpse. I know that sounds awful, and it is, but that is an accurate description.

26

"Till Death Parts Us"

January 29, 2005, started out like any other day. I got up and went for my run. When I got home, Becky sleepily walked out of her room and said, "Mom, Sunbridge called and said Dad is sick."

Déjà vu—again. I got a sick feeling as I stood there, remembering a day eighteen months ago when one phone call had suddenly changed our lives forever. My heart began to tell me that this day was going to be different.

I quickly changed and drove to Sunbridge. Apprehensively, I walked into Tim's room. There were usually signs that Tim was coming down with an infection. What was wrong, and how could I have missed it? This had come totally out of the blue!

I took one look at him and knew that this wasn't merely an infection. Something was really, really wrong with him.

He kept vomiting and the nurse told me that there was blood in it. They started giving Tim anti-nausea meds, but it didn't help, so the nurse eventually turned off his tube. I sat with him all day holding a towel up to his face. I don't even remember how many times he got sick. Later in the day, Tim began having seizures. I thought maybe he hadn't been able to keep his seizure meds down, but the nurse said she didn't think that was the case. He was given a very powerful anti-seizure medicine, and it helped a little.

I called Kay and she asked if I thought she should come. She and Jim had just left town. I said I didn't know what to tell her. I thought Tim was as bad as I had ever seen him, but he had surprised us so many times. I really didn't know. We decided that we'd keep in touch.

Dad and the kids came, and folks from church started dropping by. My mom was in the hospital herself having just had her knee replaced.

Becky and I spent the night in Tim's room. It was all so strange. He wasn't feverish and his respiratory rate, blood pressure, and heart rate were normal. We didn't know what to make of it.

On Sunday, Tim was pretty much the same. Our church was having a big party for Steve and Tami because it was the 10th anniversary of their ministry to Desert Springs. Church alumni had come in from all over for the party. One of our old friends, Jeff C., flew in from Texas, and he stopped by to see Tim. Tim was still seizing, and we began to notice that he was making some other strange movements. While Jeff sat with Tim, I got the nurse and asked her what was happening. She said she really didn't know. Later that evening, I realized what we were seeing—Tim was posturing again. That meant that something bad was happening in his brain.

The staff at Sunbridge had gotten used to Tim's extended family being nosy about his care. I read once that people do what you inspect, not what you expect, and I think that holds true when a loved one is cared for at a nursing home. The staff knew that our family or friends would be by on a daily basis to check on Tim and I think that is one reason why his care was so exemplary.

If the CNAs came in to bathe or change Tim, they often asked me to step outside. I said, "I've seen his naked bottom a lot longer than you have. I think I'll stay and give you a hand." If a nurse came into Tim's room to check his vitals, I was right beside them reading monitors. If Tim was given medication, we always asked what he was being given and why. It got to the point that the nurses walked into Tim's room and just began explaining everything.

Often, I did research on the Internet late into the night on meds that Tim was taking and treatment that he was being given. If I didn't understand something, I tracked down a nurse or a doctor and asked for explanations.

Once in a while I came across an experimental treatment for brain injuries on the Web, and the following morning I would be on the phone to Tim's doctor asking more questions. I remember reading once about how researchers were trying to use a subject's own bone stem cells to regenerate damaged brain tissue and that they were getting some hopeful results. The next day, I had talked to Dr. K. about that treatment and she just looked at me sadly and said, "I'm sorry, Carole. I just returned from a national conference on traumatic brain injuries, and we discussed all new cutting edge treatments. At this point in history, there is no cure for a traumatic brain injury or any new treatment that can grow new brain tissue."

So, that evening, when the evening shift came on, I quickly noticed that the nurse kept the monitors turned away from me and offered no numbers. He was so gentle with Tim, and afterwards, he offered to get me coffee and food. He was overly kind. Somewhat scared, I said, "You think Tim's dying, don't you?"

He couldn't say for sure, of course, but he said he was beginning to see signs of heart failure in Tim. He pointed out how cold Tim's extremities were and said that could mean Tim's organs were starting to fail. I suppose I should have called Kay, or the pastor, or somebody, but I was having trouble believing what was happening. Tim had had close shaves before and had always pulled through, so I just sat there hour after hour saying to myself, "He always turns the corner on the third day. He's going to be OK tomorrow."

On January 31 the folks from hospice came by to check on Tim. They decided to increase Tim's pain meds, and Tim's doctor agreed. Tim was still very ill, and it began to dawn on me that we might be in our last hours with him. My dad had been sitting with us, and as he got up to leave, he grabbed Tim's hand and tearfully said he was so sorry for all the trouble he'd had and that Tim had been a wonderful son-in-law.

I sent the kids home for a while and promised to call if anything happened. A little while later, Tim's nurse came in to start his tube feeding again. I couldn't believe it as we had barely got the vomiting under control. Tim was getting extra water with a syringe so he wasn't dehydrated. I questioned her why she wanted to feed Tim when he was so sick.

"The doctor told me to turn it back on."

"You know, a long time ago, the hospice nurse told me that force feeding someone at this point could do more harm than good. I don't think you should turn it on yet. Can't we just wait for a little while longer? Tim can't keep anything down. Besides, when he's been sick before, his tube was off much longer than this."

The nurse got a weird look on her face and left the room. The next thing I knew, the room was crawling with people. Hospice was trying to clarify what I had told the nurse, and the nurse was saying the doctor wanted off of Tim's case.

I couldn't believe it! The doctor was upset because I supposedly turned off Tim's tube. I said, "First of all, you guys turned off his tube. Not me. Secondly, just look at Tim. Can't you all see that he is very, very sick? He may be dying! If he was coherent and this sick, would you make him eat lunch?"

They said they wouldn't. I asked for Tim's doctor to stop by and talk to me. He hadn't been in to see Tim since Tim had fallen ill, and I wanted the doc to see for himself what kind of condition he was in. The doctor never came by, and I stood firm.

Eventually, the administrator from Sunbridge stopped by to talk with me. I explained to him that I wanted Tim's tube turned right back on as soon as he could tolerate food. He said he totally understood what I was doing and wanted to explain the doctor's behavior to me. Apparently, several years ago, Tim's doctor had gotten in some trouble and nearly lost his license over the removal of a feeding tube from one of his patients. I said this wasn't the case here, and the doc and I had always seen eye to eye on the feeding tube issue.

Then I got downright feisty. I said, "So, what you're telling me is that the doctor wants Tim's tube turned on at this time because he is afraid of getting in trouble. You mean to tell me that this has nothing to do with Tim's health and that the guy is just covering his rear end? You can tell the doctor that the only thing I care about right now is the welfare of my husband and doing what is best for him. Quite honestly, I don't think anything is going to help Tim right now, and I think pumping his stomach full of stuff will hurt him and not help him. Tonight or tomorrow, if Tim is better, I'll turn that thing on myself! But right now, LEAVE HIM ALONE!"

I walked back into Tim's room, climbed up on his bed and grabbed his cool hands. I said, "Tim, I will never, ever let anyone hurt you ever again. Now I know why I had to go through the last eighteen months. It was to prepare me for this day. Today, I don't even recognize myself. I'm a totally different person than I was a year and a half ago, and I have asked God over and over, 'Why have you made me so strong?' You know me … I'm the one who couldn't say no to the salesman on the telephone, and here I am taking on your doctor! God has given me a steel backbone so that I would fight for you today."

Eleanor (hospice nurse) and Maureen (hospice social worker) came back into the room and said they had a doctor lined up for Tim. Then they offered us a room at one of their hospice centers. They said it was a really comfortable, private place, and a much nicer environment than even Sunbridge. The kids and I could even stay in the room with Tim. I said, "Alright, that's fine, but will Sunbridge hold Tim's room for him if he starts to get better?" They assured me that they would.

So, we began making plans to move Tim. It took a few hours, but Eleanor finally came by and said Tim would be transported soon. I had sent the kids home for dinner, so I called them and told them where to meet us. Right before the van came to pick us up, I looked at Tim and noticed that his pupils had become uneven. I grabbed one of the hospice nurses, and she said very quietly, "Pressure is building up in the brain. Tim's probably got a blocked shunt."

That was something that I never expected, but it explained the lack of a fever and the bizarre symptoms Tim had been having. I realized, too, that had I taken Tim to the hospital, they might have wanted to do brain surgery on him. One thing for sure—at that moment I knew that Jesus was coming for Tim.

Eleanor was near tears as we left, and she gave me a big hug. I called Dad and Steve, and they said they'd meet us at the hospice center, which was only 15 minutes away. I sat in the dark van beside Tim, my every breath a prayer for him, for our kids, and for what was about to happen. "God, help us …"

Once we arrived at the hospice center, the nurses changed Tim into a clean shirt and tucked him into bed. As they covered him up with a patchwork quilt, I looked around at the comfortable room we had been given. Five minutes after we arrived, one of the nurses took Tim's vitals. I looked at the monitor and was so confused. "Those numbers are crazy!" I thought. "This can't be right."

Tim's pulse, which had been in the 80s and 90s since his accident, was reading under 30 bpm and slowing. The nurse couldn't even find Tim's blood pressure. I felt so scared. I asked, "What's happening?" and as I looked down at Tim, I realized he had stopped breathing.

You think that you are ready for something hard like this, that you have prepared for this moment, but you can't—not really. It is so hard, and as I stood there crying, I wished so much that the kids had made it in time.

About a minute later, one of the nurses said, "Oh my, he is such a fighter." As I looked down, Tim had begun breathing again. He was struggling so hard. At first, I felt confused, but then it hit me. Tim was waiting for the kids. I told him if he could just hang on a few minutes more that they would be there. He fought for ten more minutes. Becky, Rae, and Dan came in and joined me at his bedside. We were all crying, and I said, "Your daddy was waiting for you," and at that very moment, Tim slipped away.

The nurses said what probably happened was Tim's shunt became blocked or infected. Nothing, not even brain surgery (which I would never have subjected Tim to at that point) would have helped him. I say that God decided it was time for Tim to come home. I don't know why January 31, 2005, was THE day for Tim. Why not six months from now or six months ago? All I know is that Psalm 139 says God ordained the number of our days before we were even born.

Kathy and Glenn P. arrived just after Tim died. Then, my dad came in. A few seconds later, Pastor Steve arrived. Kathy said as she looked at the kids, particularly Rachel, she saw not only grief, but fear in their eyes.

It was a frightening moment. Even though Tim hadn't been home with us for a year and a half, he had still been there in spirit. We felt his presence, and I still acted like Tim was the head of our family. I tried to lead and guide our family following Tim's steps. I tried to think like Tim and do what he would do. Now, he was completely removed from our lives, and I was petrified at the prospect of being left to run our family alone.

We all sat there for a very long time. Tim's body still lay quietly on the bed. Finally, Steve opened up his Bible and began to read from Second Corinthians. He prayed with us and then we all got up to leave. The kids exited the room, glancing tearfully at their father as they walked away. I let everyone leave the room and then I went over to Tim and stroked his hair. Goodbye, my love ...

27

"Closure"

February 1, 2005

*For we know that if the earthly tent which is our house is torn down, we have a build-
ing from God, a house not made with hands, eternal in the heavens."*
2 Corinthians 5:1

Dear Family and Friends,
    *Last night at 7:20 p.m., after a year and a half of fighting, Timothy Robert Jones
laid aside his earthly tent and went home to be with his Lord.*
    *The kids and I are OK. It is amazing to me how you can cry quarts and quarts for
months and never run out of tears. Last night, when we finally got home, I looked at
the zombies that sort of resembled my children lying around our living room, and I
prayed, "Father, how can I help them?"*
    *I went to the closet and got a big box of photos; photos that the kids had not looked
at since their dad was hurt. I used to secretly sit in my closet some nights when I
couldn't sleep and look at these photos of Tim. It was a dumb thing to do at the time
because it was like torturing myself, looking at the photos of a healthy, vibrant, smil-
ing Tim and then to have to walk into his room and see him as he was. But I grabbed
the box, went back to the living room, and started handing out the pictures.*
    *The kids' eyes brightened and they said, "Now, this is my Dad. This is what he was
really like."*
    *We had almost forgotten the way he used to be. We sat there laughing about what
Tim was doing in this or that picture, and then the kids started talking excitedly
about where Daddy was right at that minute, who he was seeing—in person!*
    *Becky said Dad was helping to get our family's mansion all ready for us to join him
some day, to which I replied, "Oh great, that means the first thing I'll have to do when
I get to heaven is clean!" Daniel said the first thing his dad would do was figure out all
the good places to eat. They started talking about how their dad would be pulling the*

Lord and the Apostle Paul aside, asking them all sorts of tough theological questions. "Now, what exactly did you mean here? I never really understood this verse."

I guess our sadness is greatly tempered right now by our joy over Tim's deliverance. We miss him so much, but we are so happy that he is finally completely healed and home. Moments ago, we pitied Tim and thought how blessed we were to not be in his condition. Now, as Tim strolls along the streets of gold, he pities us for having to remain here a while longer.

My dad and Pastor Steve will be helping me make funeral arrangements today, so I will have someone keep you posted. Words cannot express my gratitude to all of you for holding us up for so long. God bless you.

Always in His loving grip,

Carole, Becky, Rachel, and Daniel

"Then I saw a new heaven and a new earth; for the first heaven and the first earth passed away, and there is no longer any sea. And I saw the holy city, new Jerusalem, coming down out of heaven from God, made ready as a bride adorned for her husband. And I heard a loud voice from the throne, saying, "Behold, the tabernacle of God is among men, and He will dwell among them, and they shall be His people, and God Himself will be among them, and He will wipe away every tear from their eyes; and there will no longer be any death; there will no longer be any mourning, or crying, or pain; the first things have passed away ...
Yes, I am coming quickly."Amen. Come, Lord Jesus.
Revelation 21:1–4, 22:20

The next day, Rachel and I went to clear out Tim's room. We worked quickly, trying not to dwell on what we were actually doing. At one point, I stopped and gazed at Tim's hospital bed. My grief turned to joy momentarily as I realized that Tim would never have to use that bed again.

Maureen from hospice came in and gave us a hug. She commented that she had really been touched and encouraged as she had observed our family over the past six months. She had just stopped by the nurse's station to tell them Tim had passed away. They were stunned, but she had merely wagged a finger at them and said, "See, you should have listened to his wife."

As we left Sunbridge, I stopped by the different wards where Tim had resided to thank everyone for being so compassionate to him. Tim's CNAs, especially, were such special ladies, and I wanted to tell them personally how grateful I was for them caring so lovingly for him. Everyone said they were very sorry about the incident that had occurred with Tim's doctor the previous day. They said, "It wasn't us, it was *him*." I felt a little vindicated.

As I turned to leave, I saw that Rae had been cornered by an elderly woman in a wheelchair. She had a hold on Rachel's hand, and Rae was patiently listening to her ramble on. I gently steered Rae away from her and said, "What was that all about?"

"I'm not sure. She mistook me for someone else, I guess. Then, she said she thought I worked for the President!"

We both chuckled softly. As we walked down the long hallway towards the exit, we passed by another elderly woman who looked sort of lost. Her hospital gown had gotten stuck to her under things, so she was just standing there forlornly with her diaper showing. Rae, embarrassed, looked at the ceiling as we walked by.

I put my arm around Rae and said, "God willing, you will never have to come here again."

The next few days were a blur of activity. I had been urged months ago to pre-arrange Tim's funeral, but I never had. I didn't want to face that until it was necessary.

Pastor Steve and my dad steered me in the right direction and even sat with me as we met with the funeral director. When Steve asked me if I had any ideas for the service, I said, "Tim and I actually talked about our funerals once a long, long time ago. We decided that at our funerals, we didn't even care if anybody talked about us, as long as the gospel was shared. I want you to really preach it, Steve."

I asked Larry H. and Jim H., two of Tim's closest friends, to speak at the funeral, as well as Steve. A long time ago, Becky had gotten a Nicole Nordeman track called "Legacy," and we had decided that if Tim ever died, she would sing that at his funeral. I asked Rae and Dan if they wanted to do something at the service, and they both said they didn't feel up to talking about their dad. We agreed that it would be too emotional, so Steve suggested that Dan be a pallbearer.

A couple days later, Rachel came up to me and said, "Hey, Mom. I was wondering if you'd like me to sing yours and Dad's song at the funeral." Tim and I had decided a few years back that "Dream a Little Dream of Me," sung by Mama Cass Elliot, should be "our song."

I was delighted. She said she was pretty nervous about it, and I told her to look only at me while she was singing. "Just sing to me, Rae." She started practicing, and as she sang, I began weeping. I finally started laughing and said, "Whatever you do, don't look at me when you're singing that song!"

I took the kids shopping for something appropriate to wear. Dan doesn't like to dress up, but we ended up buying him his very first suit jacket. It was navy blue, and I told him to pick out a tie to go with it. He did. It was an interesting choice. Bright, fire engine red.

We were doing OK most of the time. I'd discovered that I had several modes of operation that I switched into to cope with difficult days. Right now, I was in "taking care of business mode," and there was little time to reflect on what had happened. I was more concerned with how the kids were doing than what I was feeling. I was dreading the funeral and just wanted to get it over with.

Dear Family and Friends,

Thank you, thank you for the beautiful cards and letters, flowers and gifts that we have received since Tim's homegoing. We have enjoyed every one and have especially loved the anecdotes and stories that you have shared about Tim.

I asked Steve, our pastor, if I had to go to the visitation. He laughed and said it was expected. I was really dreading it, but it was actually a very uplifting evening. Tim looked almost as he did before his accident. Amazing.

Several friends and family members came in from out of town—some expected, some surprised us, and I greatly enjoyed the reunions. I kept thinking of the reunion Tim was experiencing in heaven.

Tim's funeral was a beautiful and fitting tribute to a wonderful man. Our good friend, Don, filmed the service for our family and friends who were unable to attend. He gave me the finished DVD last Sunday. I put the kids to bed and sat and watched the whole thing that evening. The actual day of the funeral was kind of a blur, so I appreciated hearing what was said about Tim one more time. Three of Tim's closest friends—Jim, Larry, and Steve—spoke at the funeral, and I felt so proud as they spoke of Tim's life.

At the last, my hubby was remembered not for his education or professional accomplishments (although he was accomplished), his material possessions, or the races he won or lost. He was remembered for his character and was praised for his love and devotion to his family and friends. Most of all, he was remembered for his loving relationship with God. All things that last for eternity, and I thought, "Well done, Tim."

I'd read that it helped kids in the grieving process to be involved in the planning of and even participation in the funeral. Becky ran all over in the days leading up to the funeral, helping me to make all of the arrangements. Both of our girls sang at the funeral. Rae sang our song, "Dream a Little Dream of Me," and Becky sang, "Leg-

acy," while photos of Tim's life were shown. Daniel was a pallbearer. He'd been so stoic the entire service, but after carrying his dad's casket to the hearse, he broke down and couldn't continue. Rae took his place as a pallbearer at the cemetery, and Dan walked with her and held her hand.

Tim's last hours and the ten days following were probably the most emotional moments of our lives. I remember months ago likening our situation to a deep wound that never healed. It constantly caused pain, but we had sort of adjusted to it and even learned to smile amidst it. Tim's death hit us just as if someone came along and ripped off that sticky old bandage we had used to try and cover up our unhealed wound. Ouch, that hurts! Then this someone started cleansing the wound and doctoring it—now we're talking about the kind of pain that makes you pass out. But, since then, we have noticed that while the wound still aches, the pain is not as sharp. The healing has begun, I think.

We've gotten pretty good at putting on our game faces when we walk out the door, but at home, the dam of pent-up sorrow, pain, anger, and guilt finally burst in the days leading up to Tim's funeral. I sat up many nights feebly trying to console one or another of the kids. The waves of emotion came and went, and I was beginning to feel a bit overwhelmed by the strength of the current. I prayed, "Lord, this is getting kind of scary—a little help, please," and was suddenly comforted by the thought that God hadn't sustained us for the past eighteen months only to take His hands off of us and let us fall apart now.

So, I know in the days to come, we'll be all right. We'll adjust. There will be more hard days. Probably Becky's high school graduation day in May will be a tough one, as will the kids' weddings some day. But, my hope and expectation for them is to grow up and live their lives to the fullest.

We are grateful, oh, so grateful, that Tim is out of harm's way. We can vividly imagine where he is and who he is with. We are grateful that we're no longer living in limbo and can now have a sense of closure. I half expected this trial to continue for many years, so I am grateful that in His mercy, God chose to shorten what could have been a very lengthy ordeal.

As for me ... well, I've gotten used to being by myself, although the first time somebody referred to me as a widow, I almost lost my cookies. I guess I'm single, but I sure feel married! The first few days were the toughest. It took many mornings before I could wake up and realize I didn't need to pray for Tim first thing. Everyone tells me it is normal to keep losing your train of thought and to not be able to concentrate. What a relief. Here I thought I was losing my mind as I've been walking into rooms and forgetting why I went there, missing appointments, forgetting to pay bills, driving somewhere to get something specific and coming home without it, and locking us out of the house (here's a good trick: try finding a lock smith during the Super Bowl).

These are not my usual tendencies, and it is exasperating. I'm tired, I feel old, and hey—who rubbed all the sparkle off of my life? I guess it is normal to feel like part of you has died, too. And now, we've got a whole new normal to get used to again. (There's that word normal again. I once read an anonymous quote that said, "Masquerading as a normal person day after day is exhausting." How true.) I guess I should be thankful that I have a good excuse for messing up right now.

But, we're plowing ahead. The human spirit is resilient, and providentially God has designed life to keep on going. It doesn't slow down or stop no matter what happens to any of us, and you end up getting carried along whether you want to or not. That's a good thing. We are getting back into our routine and keeping busy with productive things. Thank God for something to do.

We have you to thank for our ability to carry on. Your prayers have carried us through a very dark time. There were so many times that I wanted to scream, "I quit! This is way too hard. Nothing could be worth this pain. God can't love me if this is happening," but all I had to do was look around. I saw the love of God demonstrated every single day of this trial through the body of Christ. Because of the help and encouragement and strength that we received from you, we were able to see those kinds of thoughts for the lies that they were and reject them.

Often, I stood like one of Christ's followers described in John, chapter 6, who were tempted to walk away and leave Jesus when His teaching became too difficult or the situation got dicey. I felt like Christ kept saying, "You do not want to leave, too, do you?" and I had to answer, "Lord, to whom would I go? You have the words of eternal life! I know and believe that you are the Holy One of God."

God bless you for what you have done for us. I know that my family grew in many ways during this trial, but I think that you all did, too. We intend to follow your example because we see now that God used our trial to give the family of God an opportunity to use and develop their gifts. We would count it an honor to pray and minister to you as you have prayed and ministered to us. My family didn't go through this alone, and I want to thank you for walking this weary road with us. Most of all, I thank God that He never abandoned us.

We're going to try to stay out of trouble for a while ...

Love,
Carole and kids

Epilogue

July 2006

Two months is too little
They let him go
They had no sudden healing
To think that Providence
Would take a child from his mother
While she prays, is appalling

Who told us we'd be rescued?
What has changed and
Why should we be saved from nightmares?
We're asking why this happens
To us who have died to live?
It's unfair.

This is what it means to be held.
How it feels when the sacred is torn from your life
And you survive.
This is what it is to be loved.
And to know that the promise was
When everything fell we'd be held.

If hope is born of suffering
If this is only the beginning
Can we not wait, for one hour
Watching for our Savior?
—Natalie Grant

151

The first time I heard the lyrics to Natalie Grant's song, "Held," I was overcome with emotion. I'm too practical a person to sit around wallowing in self pity over what transpired in my life over the past three years. That would be a waste of precious time, and if there's one thing that a single parent doesn't have, it's time to waste.

Still, there are moments when I think to myself, "Is it just me, or does everyone think I got a rotten deal?"

Music is a powerful thing, but I don't normally get my theology from a song. However, the lyrics in this song are so powerful and so convicting that I find myself listening to it over and over and over again to help me remember what I so easily forget.

Who told us we'd be rescued? Why should we be saved from nightmares? Who said it was important to God that we have a large house, a large bank account, a healthy body, or a long life? Who promised us a rose garden?

I was never guaranteed lack of trouble or tribulation—I knew that. Knew that it was possible that I'd experience sorrow and pain. I even knew that God never promised that I would live forever (at least not here).

I'm not quite sure where I got the notion, though, that God could do whatever He wanted in my life, except break up my family. I deluded myself into thinking that we were immune because we were this old-fashioned, dare I say it, perfect (at least to me) little family. Surely that made it off limits.

Go ahead and line up the trials, Lord—You can give us the "financial worries trial," or the "people don't like me because I'm a Christian trial," or even the trial of cancer, but keep Your holy mitts off my man and my young'uns. There are enough messed up families out there. What You need, Lord, are more examples of godly Christian families ... or so my thinking went. I guess that's why I was so utterly shocked when Tim's accident happened. Truth be painfully told, this trial found and struck my absolute weakest point, my Achilles heel. It dealt out a death blow that should have shipwrecked my faith, destroyed my family, and left us a mess. We've all seen it happen before.

I cannot read through the pages I've written without reliving the pain that went along with Tim's accident and subsequent death. My pulse quickens, there's a tightening in my throat, and no small amount of tears. And yet, at the same time, I am overwhelmed by a sense of awe in the grace and power of God because there is absolutely no earthly reason why we responded to those dreadful circumstances the way that we did. We're flesh and blood and tears and very, very normal human beings.

Why aren't the kids and I seeing expensive therapists every other day? What reason can I give for our lack of bitterness and depression? How come we're still functioning and even thriving? Why did we remain loyal to the Holy Hands that foresaw this freight train of a nightmare heading our way and still allowed it smash into us?

I'll tell you why—because God kept His Word.

No, He never promised me continual prosperity—only that He would give me my daily bread. He never promised that my heart wouldn't break—only that He would comfort me now, and someday dry all of my tears. He never said I wouldn't walk through the valley of the shadow of death with Tim—He just promised that He'd walk with us and even carry us through.

Even now, He whispers through His Word sweet nothings to my soul; that He would be a husband to me and a father to Becky, Rachel, and Daniel; that He will meet all of our needs. He's even gone so far as to say that He will turn our sorrow into joy—now that I've got to see! And finally, He's promised that even if the entire world is shaken to its very core, He will still firmly hold its pillars in place.

A friend told me a few months ago that she admired my family. She said if anyone had a right to be bitter and to lash out at the world, it was me. She said we had made a choice to believe, to have faith, to trust, and I guess she's right, but the kids and I never looked at it that way.

For us, our response was a knee-jerk reaction to sudden calamity. It was like finding out that our ship was about to sink and reaching for the nearest life preserver. Or like being swept away by raging floodwaters and grabbing onto the nearest solidly rooted tree—with one huge difference—the life preserver and the tree firmly grabbed us back.

Rachel was musing the other day, "Mom, do you think many of the other kids that I know have had their faith really, really tested?" I said probably not that many. She continued, "You know what, Mom? When Dad got hurt I wanted to stop believing. I really, really tried to quit believing, to stop having faith in God, but I couldn't because there was nothing else."

There was nothing else but God. I know exactly how she feels.

We've been done a favor, in a way. What do you get when you strip everything away from someone and all that they have left is their relationship with the Almighty God? You get one audacious individual who is free to live like there's nothing left to lose, that's what.

I keep envisioning the mythical creature, the Hydra, from the Disney movie, *Hercules*. Boy, that thing was nearly impossible to stop! Hercules confidently whacked off its head and began walking away, positive that he'd stopped this monster once and for all. After all, if the head is gone the rest of the body can't function, right? Suddenly, he heard a noise behind him and turned around to find that two heads, not one, had grown back in its place. He sliced again and the same thing happened—more heads. Finally, his coach yelled something like, "Quit chopping off heads, you dummy!"

That's the way I picture my family. Our head was severed, but by God's grace four stronger ones have grown back to take its place. This is nothing new. In fact, it's an age-old war strategy. The enemy has tried before to destroy the body of Christ by removing the head. I can see him now ranting, "Oh, darn ... backfired again!"

Pain and suffering, toil and hardship—they're universal and common to man-kind. In the eight months since Tim died, a tsunami killed over 169,000 men, women, and children in Indonesia, one of my best friend's daughters tried to commit suicide, another dear friend's daughter has rejected Christianity to become a Muslim, and a killer hurricane ravaged the Gulf coast displacing thou-sands of Americans. The lives of many, many people were irrevocably altered or snuffed out completely. Sometimes life here on earth is a continual slap fest.

And where is God when all this happens? The same place He's always been—hanging onto us.

Each time I finish reading the book of Job I am sobered and yet strangely uplifted at the same time. I can relate to his anger and his pain and his desire for God to personally explain Himself. As Job is restored, I am comforted.

Just like Job, as quickly as our trial has begun, it has ended. This chapter in our lives is over, and as we go forward and begin a new chapter, we go forth knowing that God is with us. His ways may be inscrutable at times, but His love for us is crystal clear.

I'm hopeful that the next book that I write will begin like this line from the epilogue to the book of Job: *"The Lord blessed the latter part of Job's life more than the first."*
Job 42:12

I feel blessed—I truly do. My family is healthy, happy, goofy … normal! Daniel was a little boy when I was diagnosed with cancer. A mere nine years old. Now, at thirteen, he's a little man! His feet have gone from small boats to battleships, and he's grown right past Becky and me and is rapidly closing in on Rachel. He reminds me of Tim in so many ways. The other evening we were sitting outside the church after Awana and our friend, Emily, began teasing Daniel about a crush he has on some girl in his youth group. Emily was trying to weasel a name out of him. She finally said, "I'll give you a kiss if you tell me her name," and she leaned over and pretended to kiss Dan on the cheek.

Dan very dryly retorted in his recently deepened voice, "You missed." Our jaws dropped open in surprise, and we all burst out laughing. It was so reminiscent of Tim—it was as if he had reappeared for a moment.

Becky, who was fifteen when this season of suffering began, is now a **gorgeous**, gifted nineteen-year-old college student. She is my confidante, and together we are learning to embrace our single status, realizing that God can use us in ways right now that He couldn't if we were married.

Rachel was a tender fourteen when this all began. Now, she's a beautiful eighteen year old looking forward to college life. Her waters run deep, and she's still working through the loss of her dad. We all are in our own way, but I think that we have finally reached the point where we are ready to move on with our lives. If only God would supply a forwarding address!

Charles Spurgeon said, "Great troubles make great hearts," and I believe that God has wonderful things in store for the three of them.

As for me … life keeps me busy from day to day, but I'm still trying to figure out where I fit in. It's a couple's world, and I'm a single. I live like a single person, but I still think like a married person. Confusing! I recently ventured a toe into the dating pool briefly with an old friend and found that to be even more confusing. I told him, "I know how to be someone's wife, but I've completely forgotten how to be a girlfriend." I haven't come up with Plan B yet, and that bothers me a little as the kids flutter further from the nest.

Whoever wrote the book of Job had the advantage of knowing how that story ended. We know that life turned out beautifully for him. He was blessed and lived a long, full life. One version said he died satisfied with his days.

I don't know the ending to my story, but I have faith that it will end like Job's. I guess you'll just have to stay tuned for my next book! Hopefully, it won't include fourteen thousand sheep, six thousand camels, a thousand yoke of oxen, and a thousand donkeys … I really don't have a use for them, although I could use a new vacuum.

One last thing … everyone keeps asking how we're doing. Our answer always takes some form of: "We miss Tim, but we know that God is with us and will get us through this time. We are keeping busy, staying in God's word (and praying every day that the Lord will return soon)."

Becky walked up to me a few minutes ago with tears in her eyes and handed me a piece of paper. She'd found an old note from her dad, written probably when he was heading back to Japan for a few weeks for work during my cancer treatment. It says:

Sweetheart,
I'll miss you greatly, but God will get us through.

Stay busy, stay in the Word. See you soon.
Love, Dad

I commented through my own tears, "Wow, that is probably just what he would have said if he could have written you a note before he died.
That's exactly what we're doing, too, isn't it?"

Good advice. Or should I say, famous last words. Tim probably got his inspiration from the Lord.

"Do not let your hearts be troubled. Trust in God, trust also in me. In my Father's house are many rooms: if it were not so, I would have told you. I am going there to prepare a place for you. And if I go, and prepare a place for you, I will come back and take you to be with me that you also may be where I am ..." John 14: 1–3

Peace,
Carole

Bibliography

Arnold, Eberhard and John Howard Yoder 1984. *God's Revolution*. Mahwah, N.J.: Paulist Press.

Barclay, William 2004. *The Revelation of John*. Westminster: John Knox Press.

Bonhoeffer, Emmi 1967. Auschwitz Trials: Letters from an Eyewitness. Westminster: John Knox Press.

Bright, Bill 1965. *God loves you and has a wonderful plan for your life*. San Bernadino, Calif.: Campus Crusade for Christ International.

Chambers, Oswald 1935. *My Utmost for His Highest*. New York City: Dodd, Mead and Company.
Cox, Ella Wheeler 1888. *Poems of Pleasure*. New York City: Belford, Clarke & Co.

Crabb, Larry 2001. *Shattered Dreams*. Colorado Springs, Colo.: Waterbrook Press.

Fenelon, Francois de Salignac de La Mothe, 1973. *Let Go*. New Kensington, Pa.: Whitaker House.

Kreeft, Peter 1995. *Angels and Demons: What Do We Really Know About Them?* Ft. Collins, Colo.: Ignatius Press.

Leighton, Robert, and John Norman Pearson. 1859. *The whole works of the Most Reverend Father in God*, London: H.G. Bohn.

Lescheid, Helen Grace. "A Hope Stronger Than Our Hurts." *Discipleship Journal*, September/October 1992, Colorado Springs, Colo.: NavPress.

McDowell, Josh 1981. *The Resurrection Factor*. San Bernadino, Calif.: Here's Life Publishers.

Moore, Beth 1997. To Live is Christ: The life and Ministry of Paul. Nashville, Tenn.: Lifeway Press.

Prentiss, Elizabeth 1880. *Stepping Heavenward*. New York: Anson D.F. Randolph Co.

Sangster, Margaret 2004. *Lyrics of Love of Hearth and Home and Field and Garden*. Whitefish, Mont.: Kessinger Publishing.

Spurgeon, Charles 1995. *Morning and Evening*. Peabody, Mass.: Hendrickson Publishers.

Yancey, Philip 1977. *Where is God When It Hurts?* Grand Rapids, Mich.: Zondervan.

All scripture quoted either New American Standard or New International Version. New American Standard 1960. Grand Rapids, Mich.: World Publishing Inc. New International Version 1973. Grand Rapids, Mich.: Zondervan Publishing House.

978-0-595-51388-8
0-595-51388-3

CPSIA information can be obtained at www.ICGtesting.com
Printed in the USA
BVOW040658261011

274520BV00003B/52/P